Presidency by Plebiscite

Presidency by Plebiscite

The Reagan-Bush Era
in Institutional Perspective

Craig A. Rimmerman

Westview Press

BOULDER • SAN FRANCISCO • OXFORD

Copyright © 1993 by Westview Press, Inc.

Published in 1993 in the United States of America by Westview Press, Inc., 5500 Central Avenue, Boulder, Colorado 80301-2877, and in the United Kingdom by Westview Press, 36 Lonsdale Road, Summertown, Oxford OX2 7EW

Library of Congress Cataloging-in-Publication Data
Rimmerman, Craig A.
    Presidency by plebiscite : the Reagan-Bush era in institutional perspective / Craig A. Rimmerman.
        p.   cm.
    Includes bibliographical references and index.
    ISBN 0-8133-8333-1
    1. Presidents—United States.   2. Plebiscite—United States.
3. United States—Politics and government—1981–1989.   4. United
States—Politics and government—1989–   .   I. Title.
JK518.R56   1993
353.03'13—dc20   92-27254
                                                                                          CIP

Printed and bound in the United States of America

        The paper used in this publication meets the requirements
(∞) of the American National Standard for Permanence of Paper
        for Printed Library Materials Z39.48-1984.

10   9   8   7   6   5   4   3   2

To my father and my late mother

Contents

Tables and Figures

Acknowledgments

The successful completion of this book could not have been accomplished without the help and inspiration of numerous people.

Several of my colleagues in the Political Science Department at Hobart and William Smith Colleges offered insightful criticisms of draft chapters along the way. Peter Beckman read early drafts of Chapters 1 to 3 with his usual keen eye for detail. Micheline Ishay provided a rich contextual analysis of Chapter 5 and encouraged me to develop the argument more tightly and fully. David Ost was an inspiration in a variety of ways: he not only read and commented on the first two chapters, but he wrote to me while on research leave in Poland exhorting me to complete this book. David's letter could not have come at a better time, for he inspired me to recognize that scholars of the American political system have much to offer Eastern Europeans regarding representative government and procedural democracy in light of the massive changes experienced there in recent years.

Ryan Barilleaux, one of the finest scholars writing on the American presidency today, read the manuscript in its early stages as well as the completed draft. He offered numerous valuable suggestions for revision, which I know have improved the overall quality of this book.

My student research assistants, Rob Asher, Jamie Dixon, and Jennifer Miller, performed yeoman efforts in heeding my requests for various newspaper and journal articles pertaining to the Reagan and Bush presidencies. Dorothy Densk did a superb job in retyping the manuscript to get it in camera-ready form.

Amy Eisenberg and Jennifer Knerr at Westview Press have been supportive of this project since I proposed it to them several years ago. I could not have asked for more supportive and encouraging editors with whom to work.

This book grew out of my teaching "The American Presidency" at Hobart and William Smith Colleges. Undoubtedly, the arguments I introduce reflect the conversations I have had about the presidency with my students through the years.

And finally, I wish to acknowledge the encouragement of my parents. Much of this book was written as my mother fought a courageous but ultimately losing battle against cancer. I know that she would be very proud to see this book's completion. At a very early age, my parents instilled in me a belief in the value and the importance of a quality education. I am privileged to have had their support through the years, and it is to them that I dedicate this book.

Craig A. Rimmerman

Introduction

Presidential scholars are continually challenged in their quest to develop adequate theories of the American presidency. The absence of a clear constitutional statement of precise presidential powers guarantees changing sources of this power and promises various occupants of the Oval Office will take diverse approaches as they attempt to meet heightened citizen expectations of presidential performance. In the past thirty years, the president has been deemed a potential savior,[1] and the office has been identified as "imperial,"[2] "impossible,"[3] "tethered,"[4] "no-win,"[5] and "plebiscitary."[6] Invariably, a new president arrives in office, refutes the most recent presidential evaluation, and prompts presidential scholars to reconsider their descriptions of presidential performance. As a result, we have many descriptions of presidents but few theories of presidential performance or of the institution.[7]

Richard Waterman has argued recently that an "expectations gap" theory "has evolved in the literature over the past three decades."[8] Waterman concludes that by studying the expectations gap in detail, political scientists can bring greater clarity and conceptual rigor to understanding how presidents interact with the public over time. This book examines the broader consequences of the expectations gap for presidential governance, power, and leadership. Underlying the analysis is a concern with connecting presidential power and leadership to democratic principles and accountability.

Using the Reagan and Bush presidencies as comparative case studies, this book details the changing manifestation of presidential power in the late twentieth century. The implications of changing sources of presidential power in both domestic and foreign policy arenas for future presidents are also developed.

This book also discusses the relationship of the presidency to the American people. Norman Thomas has argued that "in studying the chief executive in a democratic society, the dynamics of the interaction between that individual and the public should be a subject of primary concern."[9] Political scientists have devoted very little attention to how the public perceives the presidency and the broader implications for presidential power, democracy, and citizenship. This relationship, rooted in the political socialization process and reinforced by the mass media, has led to hero worship and the decline of citizenship. These lofty expectations are deeply rooted in the American political culture and its fervent belief in American exceptionalism. American exceptionalism refers to the belief that the Madisonian system, characterized by "separate institutions sharing power" and widespread consensual support of the liberal capitalist values of equality of opportunity, individual achievement, and the right to acquire private property,[10] separates the United States from other countries. The president is expected to be the chief spokesperson for the political and economic system and the values emanating from that system. It is not surprising, then, that recent presidents have failed to meet these unrealistic expectations.

The analysis here extends the work of Theodore Lowi[11] in developing the consequences of the plebiscitary presidency for both the occupant of the Oval Office and the citizenry. The plebiscitary presidency is rooted in citizen support as measured through public opinion polls and reinforced through the personal link that presidents try to maintain with potential voters through television. In the absence of the strong political parties needed to build working coalitions in Congress and the electorate, presidents have turned to alternative sources of presidential power to meet the demands of the plebiscitary presidency. As Chapter 2 will make clear, presidents have received considerable support from Congress and the Supreme Court in institutionalizing the powers that they need in the attempt to meet heightened citizen expectations of presidential performance. Presidents Reagan and Bush have also recognized that successful foreign policy efforts translate into higher public opinion ratings and potentially greater success in interacting with Congress. Foreign policy concerns also allow presidents to better meet their responsibilities as the chief spokespersons of the values associated with American exceptionalism.

This is especially true given the political environment of the 1990s and beyond, one characterized by a large federal budgetary deficit combined with the difficulty of persuading the American people to accept tax increases. It suggests that presidents more frequently will be operating within the confines of resource constraints and limits on their ability to translate their domestic campaign promises into concrete public policy. This book examines how Presidents Reagan and Bush uncovered new sources of presidential prerogative power that have been institutionalized in the modern era.

Chapter 1 develops the constitutional context for the study of presidential power. It addresses two fundamental questions: Why did the framers of the Constitution create an office of the executive that is essentially open to occupants' individual interpretations of presidential power? What are the consequences of the framers' decisions for sources of presidential power today?

The historical development of the presidentially centered government of the modern, plebiscitary presidency is the focus of Chapter 2. It provides an overview of how research during the past thirty years on the American presidency has reinforced the notion that presidents are and should be the central actors in the American political system. The chapter ends by offering a critique of the postmodern presidency and argues instead that the plebiscitary presidency best captures the relationship between the presidency and the public in the modern era.

Chapter 3 offers an analysis of how Presidents Reagan and Bush have been able to govern in the absence of the cohesive political parties that are necessary to build governing coalitions. Both recognized the importance of emphasizing symbolism and a values approach in campaigning and governing as ways to promote their popularity with the press and the American people. Ronald Reagan was particularly adept in fulfilling the requirements associated with the modern, plebiscitary presidency. At the same time, both he and his successor have heightened the citizen expectations of presidential performance associated with the plebiscitary presidency as each pursued the politics of symbolism by appealing to basic American values. Finally, Chapter 3 shows that presidents who wish to have domestic policy success with Congress will need to move beyond rhetoric and a values approach and must devote renewed attention to their legislative and administrative strategies.

Reagan's and Bush's administrative strategies are the focus of Chapter 4. To what extent have these two presidents taken advantage of new sources of presidential power as they dealt with a fragmented executive branch? It is argued that the Reagan administration pursued a strategy characterized by centralization and politicization in the absence of coherent political parties. The early Bush administrative strategy represents a significant departure from that of his predecessor. George Bush failed to develop a clear ideology in his presidential campaign, and this has been reflected in his own ambiguous views on key issues, including civil rights policy, the deficit, the environment, and taxes. Unlike his predecessor, Bush hit the ground coasting, rather than running, in his efforts to establish an administrative strategy.

Chapter 5 examines several questions growing out of presidential aggrandizement of power in the foreign policy arena. What have been the consequences of the congressional reforms in the 1970s and 1980s for the role of the president and Congress in the foreign policy process? What are the values and goals that have underlaid foreign policy in the Reagan and Bush eras? Who should have the last say in directing American foreign policy and in committing American forces overseas? What is the relationship between presidential activity in foreign affairs and the plebiscitary presidency? Why do presidents turn to foreign policy in an effort to bolster their public opinion ratings and meet the demands of the plebiscitary presidency? These questions are addressed by examining specific cases growing out of the Reagan and Bush presidencies, including the 1983 invasion of Grenada, the 1983 bombing of a marine barracks in Lebanon, the 1986 bombing of Libya, the 1987 Iran-Contra affair, the 1989 invasion of Panama, and the 1991 Persian Gulf War.

Chapter 6 evaluates the president's symbolic role in the American political culture and examines the consequences of that role for the plebiscitary presidency. It is argued that principles of democratic governance are better served if political scientists challenge the lofty expectations associated with citizen and media evaluation of presidential performance. This requires that we examine what political scientists mean by presidential leadership and demystify the Oval Office. Chapter 6 concludes with a presidential evaluation scheme tied to a pedagogical strategy that takes into account institutional constraints, emphasizes the importance of democratic accountability, and roots itself in critical education for citizenship. Such a pedagogical vision is grounded in participatory democratic principles, and it is a vision that recognizes the importance of challenging traditional notions of political socialization and leadership. As educators, political scientists are uniquely positioned to offer alternative conceptions of citizenship. This is the first step toward challenging the plebiscitary presidency that has been so clearly reinforced in the Reagan and Bush eras.

Methodological Overview

Bert Rockman has argued persuasively that "studies of the presidency . . . must be driven in part by concerns that are fundamentally political-philosophical."[12] He also concludes that presidential scholars must "be conscious of what our first order assumptions about political leadership and governing are, and where they lead us in terms of conceptualizing the role of the president in the American system."[13] This book employs a comparative case study approach as it attempts to meet the challenges articulated by Rockman in his excellent overview of the presidency literature.

Using the Reagan and Bush presidencies as case studies, this work details how both men used various sources of presidential power in order to meet the demands of the plebiscitary presidency. It also attempts to place these two presidencies in their proper historical context while offering an overview of how well existing political science research has done in raising key questions and in offering the discipline and the public a better understanding of the Reagan and Bush eras. This can only be done by examining the assumptions underlying presidency research.

The comparative case study approach is a valuable vehicle for studying the American presidency because it provides a rich context for explaining existing propositions within the framework of established generalizations as well as challenging the very foundations of such generalizations. Many students of the presidency have lamented the lack of conceptual clarity associated with presidency research.[14] Those looking to this book for quantitative empirical evidence to support various claims regarding presidential power will undoubtedly be disappointed. Rather, the goal of this book is to place the presidency within broader philosophical and political concerns, exactly the kinds of concerns that should be discussed and debated in a democratic society.

This book embraces an institutional and structural approach to presidential power that raises broader questions regarding the American political system by examining the relationship between the American presidency and the citizenry. It addresses issues of executive organization, policy process, and approaches to exercising various sources of presidential power that have been further institutionalized in the Reagan and Bush eras. The hope is that the reader will come away with new questions regarding the relationship between the presidency and the citizenry and will apply these and other questions to evaluating the Reagan and Bush presidencies as well as future occupants of the Oval Office. To the extent that we begin to ask new questions, we will have made progress in developing more mature ways of assessing the role of the president in the American political system and in devising the appropriate conceptual schemes necessary for theory building in political science. Ultimately, that is the central goal of this book.

Notes

1. See Clinton Rossiter, *The American Presidency*, rev. ed. (New York: Mentor, 1960); Herbert Finer, *The Presidency: Crisis and Regeneration* (Chicago: University of Chicago Press, 1960); and Richard Neustadt, *Presidential Power: The Politics of Leadership from FDR to Carter* (New York: John Wiley and Sons, 1980).

2. See Arthur M. Schlesinger, Jr., *The Imperial Presidency* (Boston: Houghton Mifflin, 1973).

3. See Harold M. Barger, *The Impossible Presidency: Illusions and Realities of Presidential* Power (Glenview, Illinois: Scott Foresman, 1984).

4. See Thomas M. Franck, *The Tethered Presidency: Congressional Restraints on Executive Power* (New York: New York University Press, 1981).

5. See Paul C. Light, *The President's Agenda: With Notes on Ronald Reagan* (Baltimore: Johns Hopkins University Press, 1983).

6. See Theodore J. Lowi, *The Personal President: Power Invested and Promise Unfulfilled* (Ithaca: Cornell University Press, 1985).

7. See Michael Nelson, "Evaluating the Presidency," in Nelson, ed., *The Presidency and the Political System* 2nd ed. (Washington, D.C.: Congressional Quarterly Press, 1988), pp. 5-28; and Craig A. Rimmerman, "The 'Post-Modern' Presidency–A New Presidential Epoch? A Review Essay," *Western Political Quarterly* March 1991, Volume 44, Number 1, pp. 221-238 for discussions of how political scientists have attempted to conceptualize research on the presidency.

8. See Richard W. Waterman, "Editor's Introduction," in Waterman, ed., *The Presidency Reconsidered* (Itasca, Illinois: Peacock Publishers, forthcoming), p. 1.

9. Norman C. Thomas, "Studying the Presidency: Where and How Do We Go From Here?" *Presidential Studies Quarterly* 1977, Volume VII, p. 173.

10. These values comprise what Lawrence JR Herson identifies as the American Creed. See Lawrence JR Herson, *The Politics of Ideas: Political Theory and American Public Policy* (Homewood, Illinois: Dorsey Press, 1984).

11. See, in particular, Theodore J. Lowi, *The Personal President* (Ithaca: Cornell University Press, 1985).

12. Bert A. Rockman, "Presidential and Executive Studies: The One, the Few, and the Many," in Herbert Weisberg, ed., *Political Science: The Science of Politics* (New York: Agathon Press, 1988), p. 106.

13. Ibid., p. 108.

14. See, for example, Stephen J. Wayne, "Approaches," in George C. Edwards and Stephen J. Wayne, eds., *Studying the Presidency* (Knoxville: University of Tennessee Press, 1983), p. 17.

1

Constitutional Perspectives on Presidential Power

Americans, it is often said, have no state religion: they have instead a cult of the Constitution. All things surrounding the writing of the Constitution have received veneration from later generations.
—Lawrence JR Herson, *The Politics of Ideas: Political Theory and American Public Policy*

The Constitution occupies an anomalous role in American cultural history. For almost two centuries it has been swathed in pride yet obscured by indifference: a fulsome rhetoric of reverence more than offset by the reality of ignorance.
—Michael Kammen, *A Machine That Would Go of Itself*

The vexing issue of executive power proved to be a major stumbling block at the Constitutional Convention. For the constitutional framers, the precise distribution of powers among the executive, legislative, and judicial branches was a continual source of debate and intrigue. This chapter begins with the assumption that in order to evaluate the sources of presidential power in the contemporary era, it is first necessary to consider the constitutional context for the development of that power. Given the context of the times and their own experiences, the framers created a stronger executive than one might have predicted at the outset of the convention. Yet by itself, the presidency is weak because it lacks the clear constitutional powers that provide authority for presidential responsibility and decisionmaking, especially in the domestic policy arena. Presidents have recognized through the years that the framers' lasting legacy has been a framework for government rooted in separate institutions sharing powers. In the absence of clearly articulated and strong constitutional powers, presidents have turned to other sources of power.[1] These newly found sources are the subjects of this book. But before new sources of presidential power can be outlined, we must first examine the intent of the framers in light of the proceedings at the Constitutional Convention, and Madison's own notes as well as *The Federalist Papers*. While studying the original intent of the framers will not necessarily settle current constitutional debates regarding sources of presidential power, it will help to shed light on these debates and place them within their proper historical context.

The Articles of Confederation

If we are to fully understand why the framers created a unitary executive who is subject to various checks and balances, we must first understand the experiences of the thirteen states under the Articles of Confederation. The Articles of Confederation provided that the Continental Congress would be the principal governing body, with each of the thirteen states having one vote. The Congress, then, was given the "right and power" on paper "to determine peace and war; settle disputes and differences between the states; regulate the alloy and value of coins struck by the government and the states; appoint a committee to manage the general affairs of the United States when Congress was in recess; and appoint one of its members to preside."[2] From the beginning, Congress had assumed the power of the executive.[3] The framers expected Congress to play the key role in the policymaking process as a basis for republican government. It is not surprising, given revolutionary mistrust of executive authority and strong government, that the framers rejected a strong executive. Yet this distribution of power did prompt Thomas Jefferson to lament in his *Notes on the State of Virginia* that "all the powers of government, legislative, executive, and judiciary, result to the legislative body."[4]

In practice, the Articles stymied effective action for several reasons. All decisions had to be unanimous unless there were more than seven states represented, and at least nine states were required to approve decisions that involved matters of war and peace and the appropriation of money. It was often difficult to obtain the required quorum because state governments were laggard in appointing delegates, and even when they did, the delegates were often slow in assuming their responsibilities. In the end, there were severe limits on the Congress's ability to make the timely and effective decisions needed to keep the newly created government running.[5] In a letter to Thomas Jefferson, George Washington described the gravity of the situation: "That something is necessary, none will deny; for the situation of the general government, if it can be called a government, is shaken to its foundation, and liable to be overturned by every blast. In a word, it is at an end; and, unless a remedy is soon applied, anarchy and confusion will inevitably ensue."[6]

Many of the framers recognized that the Articles of Confederation simply could not meet the demands of the new nation, and widespread hostility toward state legislatures was evident from 1776 through 1787. Madison was concerned, for example, that those who feared the "'overgrown and all-grasping prerogative of an hereditary magistrate' did not realize the 'danger from legislative usurpation, which, by assembling all power in the same hands, must lead to the same tyranny as is threatened by executive usurpations.'"[7]

The historical record is clear: Weakness, inefficiency, and the potential for legislative tyranny under the Articles of Confederation led the framers to move in the direction of a strong executive at the Constitutional Convention. Yet the founding fathers wished to avoid a tyrannical royal prerogative. They opted instead for a "presidency that would be strong but still limited,"[8] one rooted in Madisonian principles designed to provide system stability and "promote administrative efficiency."[9]

Madisonian Principles

To the constitutional framers, the problem of how to provide for the stability of their newly created political system was of great concern. The delegates to the Constitutional Convention confronted two major questions: (1) How can a political system be created that allows the individual the freedom and equality of opportunity[10] needed to acquire private property? In other words, what kind of political system will allow capitalism to survive? and (2) Can a stable political and economic system be created when human beings are inherently bad?

Many of the men who gathered in Philadelphia in 1786-1787 had a Hobbesian conception of human nature. Hamilton argued in *Federalist #6* that "men are ambitious, vindictive, and rapacious." Edmund Randolph warned that the stability of the political system would be threatened due to "the turbulence and follies of our constitutions." This led Elbridge Gerry to conclude that democracy was "the worst of all political evils," while Roger Sherman argued that "the people (should) have as little to do as may be about the government" and William Livingston said that "the people have even been and ever will be unfit to retain the exercise of power in their own hands."[11] Madison himself argued in *Federalist #51* that "if men were angels, no government would be necessary. If men were to govern men, neither external or internal controls on government would be necessary."

The framers' worst fears were confirmed in the fall of 1786, when Daniel Shays, a former Continental officer, led a group of western Massachusetts farmers in protesting mortgage foreclosures. Responding to Shays's Rebellion, George Washington expressed many of the framers' concerns in a letter to James Madison: "What gracious god, is man! That there should be such inconsistency and perfidiousness in his conduct? It is but the other day, that we were shedding our blood to obtain the state constitutions of our own choice and making; and now we are unsheathing the sword to overturn them."[12] Washington wrote further that if the newly created government could not control these disorders, "what security has a man for life, liberty, or property?"[13]

These concerns are also expressed in Madison's brilliant *Federalist #10*, which serves as a compelling defense of republican government. He begins with a negative conception of human nature and argues that "the latent causes of faction are sown in the nature of man." In addition, he contends that "the most common and durable source of factions has been the various and unequal distribution of property." John Diggins has argued that Madison's negative view of human nature is connected directly to his vision of government:

> Madison trusted neither the people nor their representatives because he believed that no faction or individual could act disinterestedly. Madison traced the problem of man's invirtuous conduct to the origin of factions in unequal property relations, the "natural" conditions that led man to be envious, interested, passionate, and aggressive. Convinced that the human condition was unalterable, Madison advised Americans that the Constitution's "auxiliary" precautions were essential, that the Republic would be preserved by the "machinery of government," not the morality of man.[14]

Given these assumptions, the problem, according to Madison, was how to control the factional struggles that came from inequalities in wealth. Writing well before Marx, Madison recognized that inequalities in the distribution of property could lead to the instability of the political system. Because the causes of faction are inherent in man, it would be unrealistic to try to remove them. Instead, the framers devised a government that would try to control their effects. They attempted to do so by adopting majority rule, establishing a system of separate institutions sharing powers with checks and balances, creating federalism, and allowing for only limited participation by the citizenry in periodic elections. Women and slaves were excluded from the franchise; only property holders could vote for members of the House of Representatives. Until the Seventeenth Amendment was adopted in

1913, U.S. senators were elected by state legislatures. The cumbersome electoral college was created as a result of the framers' distrust of human nature and their desire to limit popular participation by the masses.

The framers perceived that the republican principle would grant legitimacy and stability to their newly created political system. They recognized that it would be unwise and impractical to extend democracy too broadly. To the framers, the representative was to play two key roles: He was to represent sectional and other interests in the national decisionmaking process by mediating competing claims, and he was to mediate and moderate the passions of the mob.[16] Accountability would be provided for by establishing a system of periodic elections where qualified citizens could choose their representative. Benjamin Barber concludes that representative government promised the possibility of system stability by emphasizing "popular control and wise government, self-government, accountability, and centripetal efficiency."[16]

Having outlined the values and assumptions underlying the Madisonian framework, we are now ready to connect these themes to an analysis of constitutional sources for presidential power.

The Framers and the Presidency

Notes taken at the Constitutional Convention reveal that the presidency proved to be a major stumbling block for the Framers.[17] What form the presidency would take and what its relations to the other branches would be were cause for intense debate and disagreement between the two major factions at the Constitutional Convention—the Federalists and the Anti-Federalists. The debate revolved around three main issues: the question of unity in the executive branch; the method by which the executive should be chosen; and the distribution of powers between the executive and the other branches of government as well as the states.[18]

Those Federalists who participated in state ratifying conventions "stressed both the virtues of the presidency and the restraints that the Constitution placed upon the office." They relied on the writings of Alexander Hamilton, who argued on behalf of a strong executive in the *Federalist*.[19] For Alexander Hamilton, "energy in the executive [was] a leading character in the definition of good government."[20] Hamilton called for a unified executive in order to preserve liberty. With this in mind, Hamilton looked to the British model because it provided an example of strong executive prerogative.[21] James Wilson also consistently made the case for a strong and independent executive; unity in the executive, he concluded, "would be the best safeguard against tyranny" instead of "being the foetus of monarchy."[22]

The Anti-Federalists feared that a strong national government would infringe on the rights and liberties of the state legislatures.[23] Those calling for a plural executive were concerned that unity in the executive would promote monarchy. Randolph, for one, felt that the "vigor, dispatch, and responsibility" of the executive could be carried out as well by three men, as by one. To Randolph, the independence of the executive was of the utmost importance, and it could only be insured in the plural form.[24] The Anti-Federalists feared that a strong presidency with an aristocratic Senate would move the new nation toward a monarchy.[25] Finally, they accepted a compromise proposal that attempted to balance the states' rights with the sovereignty of the national government.

Several specific proposals were set forward to meet the aforementioned concerns. The Virginia plan, proposed by Randolph, "recommended instituting a national executive 'with power to carry into affect the national laws.'" In this plan, the executive would be chosen by the national legislature.[26] The New Jersey plan, on the other hand, responded to the concern of the smaller states that too much power concentrated in the executive branch could threaten liberty. William Paterson of New Jersey proposed that Congress should have the right to tax and regulate state commerce, "but it would retain a single-house legislature in which all states, regardless of size, would have the same vote."[27] The New Jersey plan provided for a plural executive chosen by Congress and a Supreme Court appointed by the executive. Much to the dismay of Alexander Hamilton and James Wilson, the plural executive concept received considerable attention at the convention. Roger Mason, for example, asked these questions:

> If the Executive is vested in three persons, one chosen from the Northern, one from the Middle, and one from the Southern States, will it not contribute to quiet the minds of the people and convince them that there will be proper attention paid to their respective concerns? Will not three men so chosen bring with them, into office, a more perfect and extensive knowledge of the real interests of this great Union?[28]

A committee of eleven was chosen to offer a compromise. The Connecticut Compromise, so named due to the active role played by the Connecticut delegation, recommended a bicameral legislature with one branch providing equal votes to the states and the other based on population.[29] The executive would be occupied by a single individual, with support from a cabinet, and would be subject to numerous checks and balances. Yet as Bessette and Tulis conclude, "the architects of the presidential office consciously rejected a plural executive or one checked by an executive council in order to ensure that the presidency would possess those capacities which, they believed, characterized every well-constructed executive branch: decision, activity, secrecy, and dispatch."[30]

It is interesting to note that the expectation that George Washington would be the first chief executive had a profound influence on the structure of the office. The historian Hugh Brogan concludes that the trust Washington inspired encouraged the framers to accept a one-person presidency: "Had Washington died suddenly in the middle of the convention Wilson might have got his way and the United States have acquired a three- or four-man executive, like the Directory in Revolutionary France.[31]" Washington's reluctance to assume the presidency for a lengthy period also forced the framers to confront how the executive was to be chosen. This issue proved difficult to resolve. Some framers favored popular election, others advocated election by the national legislature, and a third group called for election by an electoral college.[32] This electoral college was to be composed of "a council of wise men" who would be chosen by state legislatures and would have a number based on each state's total membership in the House of Representatives and the Senate. As Lawrence Herson suggests, the framers' intent in creating the electoral college was clear: "to mediate between direct majority rule and the eventual selection of the president."[33] They thought that the Senate would ultimately choose the president because after Washington was chosen, no future candidate would likely gain the necessary majority of the electoral college vote.[34]

Having settled the question of the structure of the Presidency, the framers had to resolve the powers to be accorded the incumbent. The development of presidential power must be seen within the broader context of Madisonian principles and capitalist values. In their effort to provide for system stability, the constitutional framers used the language of Newtonian physics[35] and were guided by the philosophy articulated in Baron de Montesquieu's *The Spirit of Laws*.[36] To Montesquieu, "when the legislature and executive powers are united in the same person, or in the same body of magistracy, there can be then no liberty."[37] Following Montesquieu, Madison argues in *Federalist #47* that "the accumulation of all powers, legislative, executive, and judiciary, in the same hand . . . may be justly pronounced the very definition of tyranny." The dilemma for the framers, then, was how to create a "strong republican executive."[38] They attempted to do so in several ways.

At the heart of the Madisonian system is the differentiation of powers and structures in the form of three distinct branches of government. The legalistic interpretation of power has stressed "parchment distinctions," while political scientists, following Neustadt, have argued that the Constitution creates "separate institutions sharing power."[39] The latter interpretation is probably most accurate and most useful for understanding the changing sources of presidential power through the years.[40] In the absence of clear constitutional powers in, for example, the foreign policy arena, presidents have turned to "extraformal" powers in order to meet heightened expectations of presidential performance.[41] Hamilton's argument that the framers gave Congress and the executive "joint possession" of the war-making and treaty-making powers is particularly relevant here. The president is responsible for commanding the armed forces, but Congress provides the funding. Congress is required to formally declare war, but the president has the constitutional authority to employ the weapons of war. All presidential appointees in the form of ambassadors, special negotiators, and other U.S. representatives to foreign governments must be confirmed by Congress. The Constitution also grants the executive and legislative branches the powers to make the laws as well as staff the administration.

In their effort to calm the prevailing fear of monarchy, the framers defined presidential powers imprecisely and were purposely vague. Article II, section 2.1 mandates that "the Executive power shall be vested in a president of the United States of America." This sentence has been interpreted in two ways. Some have argued that the framers intended for the president to head the executive branch. A far more expansive and common interpretation gives a broad, undefined authority to the president, an authority that provides presidents with the opportunity to use various prerogative powers.[42] It is important to recognize, however, that the framers rejected the Lockeian notion of executive prerogative powers. According to Richard Pious, "presidents who claim constitutional authority to unilaterally make the most important domestic and national security policies in effect institute prerogative government." The exercise of presidential prerogative power is characterized by the following features: Presidential decisions are often made in secrecy, without consultation of Congress, and are presented to the public only after the decision has been made; and, the decisions are often carried out by executive subordinates, with overall implementation managed by the White House rather than specific departments.[43] The founding fathers did not write such executive power explicitly into the Constitution. Given their negative view of human nature and their experiences with monarchy, they knew that responsible and accountable government could not be preserved if such power was placed solely in the hands of the executive. Because the Constitution itself is so unclear regarding precise presidential powers, however, presidents have turned to alternative sources of presidential prerogative power to meet heightened citizen expectations in the modern era. The sources of these powers are discussed later in this book.

Few clear powers were assigned to the President in the domestic policy arena, save for vetoing legislation (which can be overridden), using the pocket veto (which cannot be overridden), reporting to Congress on the State of the Union, and faithfully executing the laws. The Constitution is particularly confusing in the foreign policy arena and fails to make the clear distinctions between "the right to make war and the ability to get the men and money required to carry it out."[44] As will be argued in Chapter 5, this has led to considerable conflict between Congress and the president through the years. In the end, the framers felt that presidential power "should be a broadly discretionary residual power available when other governmental branches failed to meet their responsibilities or failed to respond to the urgencies of the day."[45]

The framers hoped that by separating institutions, grounding them in different constituencies, and requiring the sharing of key powers, they would be able to prevent the oppressive use of power by any one branch of government. In justifying this scheme, William Randolph argued that "where the liberties of the people are to be preserved, and the laws well administered, the executive, legislative and judicial, should ever be separate and distinct, and consist of parts, mutually forming a check upon each other."[46] Madison defended the need for overlapping powers and claimed that this important scheme was far better than the Anti-Federalist demand that powers be divided clearly among the various branches of government.[47] Others, however, believed that this sharing of powers, particularly between the Senate and the president, was the "fatal defect" in the newly created system.[48] James Wilson decried the possibility of a legislative despotism,[49] and Alexander Hamilton warned that if the states gained too much power at the expense of the national government, then "the national government cannot long exist when opposed by such a weighty rival."[50]

Historical practice provides evidence that the framers' system has forestalled radical policy change and served as the basis for our incremental policy process. In a system of shared powers, presidents must labor mightily to build the bipartisan governing coalitions needed to enact public policy. Some view this as a positive legacy of the framers' efforts. A second perspective suggests, however, that separating institutions and requiring the sharing of key powers among branches has led frustrated presidents to bypass the process altogether and to exercise presidential prerogative power under the guise of national security or emergency concerns. Presidential actions in Vietnam, Cambodia, the Watergate affair, and the Iran-Contra episode are examples of the latter perspective. In this sense, then, the framers' efforts have been undermined to the extent that principles of account-ability and representative government are threatened by presidents who assert presidential power in the absence of a clear demarcation of presidential and congressional powers, especially in the foreign policy arena.

The framers also built in checks and balances to coincide with their system of shared powers. Their vision was to strike a balance between competing interests in a society that would foster overall system stability. The key was to strike the proper balance between the desire for liberty and the need for authority,[51] while institutionalizing conflict among the branches. They attempted to do so in the following ways:

1. by creating separate constituencies for Presidential, Senatori-al, and Representative elections;
2. by providing differing tenures of office;
3. by creating a bicameral legislature;
4. by having constituencies that are distinct in geographic size;
5. by having presidential control over appointments with senatorial confirmation;
6. by allowing a Presidential veto of congressionally passed legislation;
7. by providing federalism, which allowed the framers to deal with the problem of having the republican form of govern-ment over a vast authority and divided political authority between two levels of government—national and state.[52]

This complicated checks and balances system has led some to question whether the system has been so successful that few timely policies can be passed and implemented.[53]   Hamilton, for example, anticipated many late twentieth century criticisms of our incremental Madisonian policy process when he warned of the dangers associated with minority tyranny:

> If a pertinacious minority can control the opinion of a majority, respecting the best mode of conducting it, the majority in order that something may be done must conform to the views of the minority; and thus the sense of the smaller number will overrule that of the greater and give a tone to the national proceedings. Hence, tedious delays; continual negotiation and intrigue; contemptible compromises of the public good.[54]

Echoing Hamilton's concern, the historian Richard Hofstadter argued that the end result of the framers' efforts is "a harmonious system of mutual frustration."[65]

The Constitution and Changing Sources of Power

It is perhaps surprising, given their deep distrust of unchecked executive power and their Hobbesian conception of human nature, that the framers created a single executive with a modicum of domestic and foreign policy powers. The convention's records reveal little evidence, however, that the framers considered the consequences of their decisions in 1787 for future generations. Some have pointed out that the framers' true genius is reflected in their decision not to identify presidential powers specifically and in full detail.[66] In the twentieth century, presidential powers derive from those asserted by successive incumbents in the face of an acquiescing Congress. A lasting legacy of the framers of the Constitution is that individual presidents have the freedom to make the choices regarding the opportunities and constraints available to them in their exercise of presidential power. Yet in their efforts to promote liberty and impede majority tyranny, the architects of the Constitution may have performed their task too well. Nowhere is this more evident than when a president attempts to sustain the momentum of his honeymoon period by building the governing coalition that he needs in Congress and in the electorate to translate his domestic and foreign policy campaign promises into concrete public policy. Our incremental Madisonian policy process has made it increasingly difficult for presidents to govern in a time of resource scarcity.

As the Reagan experience suggests, presidents have turned to the use of values and the symbolism of the Oval Office to rally public support for their presidency in the absence of governing coalitions. This, too, has its roots in the Constitutional Convention of 1787 and the historical development of American exceptionalism. The story of the Convention was the ability of the Federalists and the Anti-Federalists to agree upon a final document after lengthy debate and compromise. Ultimately, however, the two sides were able to reach agreement because, in the words of Hugh Brogan, "they both encouraged the economic individualism and the national ambitions of the new republic."[67] Michael Kammen labels this propensity to disagree over procedural issues within the broader context of adhering to basic American values "conflict within consensus."[68] This widespread agreement on basic American values, including individualism, equality of opportunity, limited government, free enterprise, and republican-ism,[59] has fostered overall system stability. It is also the basis of American exceptionalism, which has been an important source of presidential power through the years.

Chapter 2 traces the development of presidential power by placing the relationship between the presidency and the public in historical context and by discussing the changing sources of presidential power. To understand the rise of the plebiscitary presidency and the consequences of this development for presidential power in the modern era, Chapter 2 examines the presidency of Franklin Delano Roosevelt.

Notes

1. See Lester G. Seligman and Cary R. Covington, *The Coalitional Presidency* (Chicago: Richard Irwin, 1989), p. 94.

2. Benjamin I. Page and Mark P. Petracca, *The American Presidency* (New York: McGraw Hill, 1983), p. 21.

3. See Richard B. Morris, "The Origins of the American Presidency," in Michael R. Beschloss and Thomas E. Cronin, eds., *Essays in Honor of James MacGregor Burns* (Englewood Cliffs, New Jersey: Prentice Hall, 1989), pp. 27-31, for an intensive discussion of this important point.

4. Quoted in Donald L. Robinson, *"To the Best of My Ability": The Presidency and the Constitution* (New York: Norton, 1987), p. 43.

5. Page and Petracca, 1983, p. 21.

6. Max Farrand, ed., *The Records of the Federal Convention of 1787*, Volume I (New Haven: Yale University Press, 1966), p. 31.

7. C. Herman Pritchett, "The President's Constitutional Position," in Thomas Cronin, ed., *Rethinking the Presidency* (Boston: Little, Brown, and Co., 1982), p. 117.

8. Arthur Schlesinger, Jr., *The Imperial Presidency* (Boston: Houghton Mifflin, 1973), p. vii.

9. Louis Fisher, *The Politics of Shared Power: Congress and the Executive* (Washington, D.C.: Congressional Quarterly Press, 1987), p. 2.

10. See Seymour Martin Lipset, *The First New Nation* (New York: Norton, 1979).

11. Richard Hofstadter, "The Founding Fathers: An Age of Realism," in Robert Horwitz, ed., *The Moral Foundations of the American Republic*, 3rd ed. (Charlottesville: University of Virginia Press, 1986), p. 63.

12. James MacGregor Burns, *The Power to Lead: The Crisis of the American Presidency* (New York: Simon and Schuster, 1984), pp. 105-106.

13. Burns, 1984, p. 106.

14. John Patrick Diggins, *The Lost Soul of American Politics: Virtue, Self-Interest, and the Foundations of Liberalism* (Chicago: University of Chicago Press, 1984), p. 53.

15. Benjamin Barber, "The Compromised Republic: Public Purposelessness in America," in Richard Hofstader, ed., *The Moral Foundations of the American Republic*, 3rd ed. (Charlottesville: University of Virginia Press, 1986), p. 48.

16. Barber, 1986, p. 48.

17. See James Madison, *Notes on Debates in the Federal Convention of 1787 Reported by James Madison* (New York: Norton, 1987).

18. Robinson, 1987, p. 68.

19. Sidney M. Milkis and Michael Nelson, *The American Presidency: Origins and Development, 1776-1990* (Washington, D.C.: Congressional Quarterly Press, 1990), p. 59.

20. Alexander Hamilton, *Federalist #70*, p. 423.

21. Christopher H. Pyle and Richard M. Pious, *The President, Congress, and the Constitution* (New York: The Free Press, 1984), p. 48.

22. Madison, 1987 [1787], p. 46.

23. Pyle and Pious, 1984, p. 48.

24. Farrand, ed., 1966, Volume I, p. 74.

25. See Milkis and Nelson, 1990, pp. 58-59, for a good discussion of the Anti-Federalist critique of the presidency.

26. Morris, 1989, p. 287.

27. James MacGregor Burns, J. W. Peltason, and Thomas E. Cronin, *Government by the People*, 13th National ed. (Englewood Cliffs, New Jersey: Prentice Hall, 1987), p. 13.

28. Farrand, ed., 1966, Volume I, p. 113.

29. See Morris, 1989 and Clinton Rossiter, *1787: The Grand Convention* (New York: Norton, 1966).

30. Joseph M. Bessette and Jeffrey Tulis, "The Constitution, Politics, and the Presidency," in Bessette and Tulis, eds., *The Presidency in the Constitutional Order* (Baton Rouge: Louisiana State University Press, 1981), p. 17.

31. Hugh Brogan, *The Longman History of the United States of America* (New York: William Morrow, 1985), p. 216.

32. Minor Myers, Jr., *Liberty Without Anarchy: A History of the Society of the Cincinnati* (Charlottesville: University of Virginia Press, 1983), p. 99.

33. Lawrence JR Herson, *The Politics of Ideas: Political Theory and American Public Policy* (Chicago: Dorsey, 1984), p. 72.

34. Richard M. Pious, *The American Presidency* (New York: Basic Books, 1979), p. 28.

35. For a thoughtful discussion of the influence of Newton on the framers, see James Farr, "Political Science and the Enlightenment of Enthusiasm," *American Political Science Review* March 1988, Volume 82, #1, pp. 51-71.

36. For an alternative explanation that emphasizes the influence of the Scottish enlightenment thinkers, including Hutcheson and More, on the constitutional framers, see Garry Wills, *Explaining America: The Federalist* (Garden City, New York: Doubleday, 1981) and Wills, *Inventing America: Jefferson's Declaration of Independence* (New York: Random House, 1979).

37. Quoted in Pyle and Pious, 1984, p. 10.

38. Ruth Weissbourd Grant and Stephen Grant, "The Constitution, Politics, and the Presidency," in Joseph M. Bessette and Jeffrey Tulis, eds., *The Presidency in the Constitutional Order* (Baton Rouge: Louisiana State University Press, 1981), p. 31.

39. Jeffrey Tulis, *The Rhetorical Presidency* (Princeton: Princeton University Press, 1987), p. 43.

40. Louis Fisher argues, on the other hand, that "although powers are not separated in a pure sense, it does not help to characterize the federal government as a 'blend of powers.' The branches have distinctly different responsibilities, practices, and traditions" [p. 15]. Yet even he admits that in many cases we are dealing with "mere shades of difference," and there has never been crisp demarcations among the three branches [p. 99]. See Louis Fisher, *Constitutional Conflicts between Congress and the President* (Princeton, New Jersey: Princeton University Press, 1985).

41. Barbara Kellerman, *The Political Presidency: Practice of Leadership* (New York: Oxford University Press, 1984), p. 15.

42. Barbara Hinckley, *Problems of the Presidency: A Text with Readings* (Glenview, Illinois: Scott Foresman, 1985).

43. Pious, 1979, p. 47.

44. Frank Kessler, *The Dilemmas of Presidential Leadership: Of Caretakers and Kings* (Englewood Cliffs, New Jersey: Prentice Hall, 1982), p. 170.

45. Thomas E. Cronin, *The State of the Presidency*, 2nd ed. (Boston: Little, Brown, 1980), p. 120.

46. Farrand, ed., 1966, Volume III, p. 108.

47. See Madison, *Federalist #10*; and for a thoughtful interpretation of Madison's efforts, see Louis Fisher, "The Doctrine of Separated Powers," in Thomas E. Cronin, ed., *Rethinking the Presidency* (Boston: Little, Brown, and Co., 1982), p. 155.

48. Robinson, 1987, p. 90.

49. See Farrand, ed., 1966, Volume I, p. 254, for a discussion of Wilson's views.

50. Farrand, ed., 1966, Volume I, p. 296.

51. Rossiter, 1966, p. 64.

52. Robert Dahl, *A Preface to Democratic Theory* (Chicago: University of Chicago Press, 1956), p. 14 and Herson, 1984.

53. See James MacGregor Burns, *The Power to Lead: The Crisis of the American Presidency* (New York: Simon and Schuster, 1984) and James L. Sundquist, *Constitutional Reform and Effective Government* (Washington, D.C.: Brookings Institution, 1985).

54. Hamilton, *Federalist #22*, p. 148.

55. Richard Hofstadter, *The American Political Tradition* (New York: Alfred A. Knopf, 1948), p. 51.

56. See, for example, Gregor Reinhard, "The Origins of the Presidency," in David C. Kozak and Kenneth N. Ciboski, eds., *The American Presidency: A Policy Perspective from Readings and Documents* (Chicago: Nelson Hall, 1985), p. 2.

57. Brogan, 1985, p. 265.

58. Michael Kammen, *A Machine that Would Go By Itself: The Constitution in American Culture* (New York: Alfred A. Knopf, 1986).

59. For a thoughtful discussion of the implications of widespread attachment to these values for community, see Robert N. Bellah, Richard Madsen, William Sullivan, Ann Swidler, and Steven M. Tipton, *Habits of the Heart: Individualism and Commitment in American Life* (New York: Harper and Row, 1985). See also, Lipset, 1979, for a discussion of the historical and constitutional context for the development of these values.

2

The Rise of the
Plebiscitary Presidency

The Constitutional framers would undoubtedly be disturbed by the shift to the presidentially centered government that characterizes the modern era. Their fear of monarchy led them to reject the concept of executive popular leadership. Instead, they assumed that the legislative branch would occupy the central policymaking role and would be held more easily accountable through republican government.

Congress has failed, however, to adhere to the framers' intentions and has abdicated its policymaking responsibility. The legislature, with support from the Supreme Court, has been all too willing to promote the illusion of presidential governance by providing the executive with new sources of power, including a highly developed administrative apparatus, and by delegating authority for policy implementation to the executive through vague legislative statutes.

This chapter traces the development of presidential power sources by examining the changing role of the presidency in the American political system as it is reflected in two distinct historical periods: the traditional and modern eras. The evolution of presidential power sources can be evaluated according to the interaction between the president, Congress, and the Supreme Court; the size and characteristics of the presidency; the relationship of the citizenry to the office of the presidency; and the role of the presidency in the American political culture.

The president-centered government of the modern, plebiscitary era draws much of its power and legitimacy from the popular support of the citizenry, support that is grounded in the development of the rhetorical presidency and the exalted role of the presidency in the American political culture. Theodore Lowi is surely on target when he identifies "the refocusing of mass expectations upon the presidency" as a key problem of presidential governance since Franklin Delano Roosevelt and as a problem associated with the rise of the plebiscitary presidency.[1]

The plebiscitary presidency is characterized by the following: presidential power and legitimacy emanates from citizen support as measured through public opinion polls; in the absence of coherent political parties, presidents forge a direct link to the masses through television; and structural barriers associated with the Madisonian governmental framework make it difficult for presidents to deliver on their policy promises to the citizenry.[2] The framers of the Constitution would hardly have approved of these developments, for they had no intention of establishing a popularly elected monarch.[3] Moreover, the nature of the governmental framework that they created actually prevents occupants of the Oval Office from meeting the heightened citizen expectations associated with the plebiscitary presidency in terms of concrete public policy, especially in the domestic policy arena. This has become particularly clear in the modern era as presidents confront a more fragmented and independent legislature, a decline in the importance of the political party as a governing and coalition-building device, an increase in the power of interest groups and political action committees that foster policy fragmentation, and a bureaucracy that resists centralized coordination. In order to understand these important systemic changes and analyze what they portend for future presidents, we must first place the development of changing sources of power in historical context.

Congressional Government in the Traditional Era

Throughout much of the nineteenth century, a passive president in domestic policymaking was deemed both acceptable and desirable.[4] Congress took the lead in formulating public policy initiatives and expressed outright hostility toward presidential suggestions that particular legislation should be introduced. In fact, early in the nineteenth century it was commonly believed that the president should not exercise the veto to express policy preferences.[5] The president's primary responsibility was to faithfully execute the laws passed by Congress. For the occupants of the Oval Office in the traditional period, the Constitution imposed "strict limitations on what a President could do."[6] The constitutional separation of powers was taken seriously by all parties, and the prevailing view regarding the proper role of government was "the best government governed least."[7] As opposed to the presidential government of the modern period, the traditional era was characterized by congressional leadership in the policy process.

In the foreign policy arena, however, the president did establish himself through the war-making power.[8] Yet even here the president was restrained when compared to the occupants of the Oval Office in the twentieth century. A prevailing view in the nineteenth century was that the president should avoid involvement with foreign nations, although negotiation with foreign countries was occasionally required. The first president to travel abroad on behalf of the United States was Theodore Roosevelt. Prior to the twentieth century, some members of Congress even argued that the president lacked the necessary legal authority to travel in this manner.[9]

Presidential speechmaking also reflected the largely symbolic chief-of-state roles played by presidents in the traditional era. Jeffrey Tulis's content analysis of presidential speeches reveals that presidents rarely gave the kind of official popular speeches that characterize speech-making in the modern era. When speeches were given, they were considered "unofficial," and they rarely contained policy pronounce-ments. Tulis concludes that William McKinley's rhetoric was represen-tative of the century as a whole: "Expressions of greeting, inculcations of patriotic sentiment, attempts at building 'harmony' among the regions of the country, and very general, principled statements of policy, usually expressed in terms of the policy's consistency with that president's understanding of republicanism."[10] Virtually all presidents of the time adhered to the same kind of presidential speechmaking. The only exception was Andrew Johnson, who attempted to rally support for his policies in Congress through the use of fiery demagoguery. Johnson's "improper" rhetoric fueled his impeachment charge; yet it is this same kind of rhetoric that today is accepted as "proper" presidential rhetoric.

The reserved role played by the president in the nineteenth century was clearly in keeping with the intention of the constitutional framers. As Chapter 1 suggests, they feared that presidential demagoguery could threaten the stability of the political system by inciting the passions of the citizenry. They also stressed the important role that members of Congress should play in the policymaking process. In sum, presidents in the nineteenth century were expected to exercise only those powers stated clearly in the Constitution. Yet as the United States headed into its second full century, this situation was to change, as congressional government began to yield to the presidentially centered form of governance that has characterized the modern period.

Why the Plebiscitary Presidency?

Students of the presidency have identified a number of factors that have led to the development of the modern, personal, plebiscitary presidency as we know it today. The personal presidency is "an office of tremendous personal power drawn from the people—directly through Congress and the Supreme Court—and based on the new democratic theory that the presidency with all powers is the necessary condition for governing a large, democratic nation."[11] Its development is rooted in changes in presidential rhetoric, the efforts of the progressive reformers of the early twentieth century, the Great Depression and Franklin Delano Roosevelt's New Deal, the role of Congress in granting the executive considerable discretionary power, and Supreme Court decisions throughout the twentieth century that have legitimated the central role that the president should play in the domestic and foreign policy arenas.

The Development of the Rhetorical Presidency

The development of the rhetorical presidency in the twentieth century signified presidential recognition of a new source of prerogative power that serves as the basis for the personal, plebiscitary presidency today. Presidential willingness to secure popular and legislative support for public policy initiatives through speechmaking and "going public" constituted "a fundamental transformation of American politics that began at the outset of the twentieth century."[12] With the presidencies of Theodore Roosevelt and Woodrow Wilson, the idea of the public presidency began to gain acceptance. Roosevelt identified the presidency as the office of the people and set the foundation for the development of the plebiscitary presidency. Wilson extended Roosevelt's practices by rejecting congressional government and arguing that presidents must exercise their roles as important symbols of the nation. Wilson believed that presidents could only claim the public support needed to translate campaign promises into concrete public policy if they emphasized patriotism and the importance of building national consensus.[13] He attempted to accomplish all of these goals by introducing a fundamental transformation in presidential rhetoric that was characterized by less rhetoric directed to Congress but more to the larger citizenry, greater emphasis on speeches and less on written statements, and changes in the structure of argumentation to a more "inspirational and policy-stand rhetoric."[14] It took the presidency of Franklin Delano Roosevelt, however, to fully develop these rhetorical techniques and to set the groundwork for "going public" that character- izes presidential communications today. FDR used radio to manipulate public opinion and garner public support for his New Deal policy initiatives. His fireside chats proved to be an important tool and an impressive use of presidential prerogative power to rally public support for his policies in a time of national emergency. In the words of William

Leuchtenburg, aspirants to the White House have truly been "in the shadow of FDR" as they attempt to rally public support for their policies through effective use of the media.[15]

Progressive Reformers and the
Rise of Presidential Government

With the presidencies of Theodore Roosevelt and Woodrow Wilson and the rise of the progressive movement in American politics, the prevailing view that the president should play a limited role in the legislative process began to change. The progressive movement embraced a managerial approach to government that emphasized increased citizen participation in political parties and a commitment to principles of efficiency and scientific expertise. Progressive reformers called for greater presidential involvement in the legislative process because the executive better represented the public interest than did Congress. From the vantage point of the progressive reformers, the presidency was best situated to make up for the failure of the legislature to protect the public interest.[16]

The progressive reformers' desire for a revitalized executive lost steam in the 1920s with the Harding, Coolidge, and Hoover administrations.[17] The presidency of Franklin Delano Roosevelt and the federal government's response to the New Deal, however, rekindled the progressive spirit. According to Fred Greenstein, "FDR promptly established the practice of advocating, backing, and engaging in the politics of winning support for legislation. By the end of his long tenure, presidential activism had come to be taken for granted, if not universally approved."[18] In the end, many have come to revere FDR for the leadership that he exercised in enlarging the presidency, expanding the domain of the federal government, and providing hope to the citizenry as they confronted the suffering of the Great Depression.[19] The problem for Roosevelt's successors is that they have found it difficult to approach the standards set by FDR. As a result, both scholars and citizens have identified "failed" presidencies without recognizing that the highly fragmented and incremental political system framed by the Constitution deters sustained popular presidential leadership of Congress. In addition, it is often forgotten that despite Roosevelt's success in passing a flood of legislation during the first hundred days of his administration,[20] he did suffer some major legislative setbacks (for example, having certain provisions attached to his New Deal initiatives) and was largely unsuccessful in prompting Congress to pass his major policy proposals after 1936.[21] The key to understanding Roosevelt's early policy success is to recognize the historical context of the times, FDR's own inspiring leadership, and Congress's willingness to pass legislation that "allowed the president to institutionalize his role as policy initiator."[22]   Roosevelt embraced the sources of presidential power that the progressives had hoped would insure governmental decisionmaking to protect the public interest. The lasting legacy of FDR's presidency has been the altered role of the president in the American political system and the identification of new sources of presidential power.   In the words of Harold Barger, "The Executive Branch did, in fact, take on additional major responsibilities and powers which affected every American and which made the national government increasingly more important and visible than ever before."[23]

Perhaps Roosevelt's greatest contribution to the development of presidential power was his extension of the personal, plebiscitary presidency. Theodore Lowi contends that as the national government's responsibilities grew in scope during the 1930s and 1940s, presidents needed an electoral base to support an activist presidency.[24]   While Roosevelt attempted to leave a popular base rooted in party organization, he was actually more successful in linking, in the minds of the citizenry, the office of the presidency to the personification of the values of American exceptionalism and good government. As a result, citizens have learned to evaluate the government and the president in terms of service delivery. For many Americans, "The president has become the embodiment of government."[25]   It is this development that marks the beginning of the modern presidency after 1933.

Congress, the Court, and Presidential Governance

Through congressional delegation and passive acquiescence in the face of presidential assertions of power, Congress has played a particularly important role in legitimating the president's central policymaking position. The Budget and Accounting Act of 1921 was a congressional initiative that institutionalized the president as the budget's central manager. Primacy for managing the nation's economic affairs was awarded to the president by Congress with the passage of the Employment Act of 1946. This act, which created the Council of Economic Advisers, guaranteed that presidents would be given more help (in the form of increased staffs) as they prepared their yearly economic reports to Congress.[26]

A third major development in presidential power occurred when Congress partially implemented the Brownlow recommendations under the Reorganization Act of 1939. Created by FDR in 1936 and led by Louis Brownlow, the Committee on Administrative Management (the

Brownlow Commission) concluded that "the President needs help." Their specific policy recommendations grew out of a careful review of the implementation of existing federal programs and included the following reform suggestions: (1) the creation of an executive office of the president to be staffed partially by White House aides (with a "passion for anonymity") who would be responsible for monitoring the performance of executive branch personnel; and (2) the shifting of the Bureau of the Budget to the White House so that the President could better coordinate the budget process.[27] The result of the Brownlow Commission's recommendations and congressional acceptance of the Roosevelt proposals has been a tremendous growth in the executive branch of government, growth that is reflected in the steady increase in personnel over the past half century. This has actually made it increasingly difficult for presidents to govern as they attempt to deal with the independent sources of power that characterize the bureaucracy.

Perhaps the most important abdication of congressional responsibility in the policymaking process has occurred in the form of the vague legislative statutes that emanate from Congress and that place the responsibility for policy implementation in the hands of the executive. Written in broad and vague language, this legislation affords considerable discretion to the implementing agency while insuring that individual congressional members will not be held accountable for specific policy initiatives. In this way, Congress has consistently rejected the constitutional framers' concern that it behave in an accountable and responsible manner[28] and has forced the occupant of the Oval Office to endure much of the blame.

There are several reasons Congress has abdicated its major policymaking role since 1933. The nature of the institution in terms of its 535 individual members, its unwieldy committee and subcommittee structure, and its labyrinth-like law-making process prevents Congress from responding in a timely fashion to complex policy issues with coherent national policies. Because of the incremental policy framework outlined in the Constitution, Congress also lacks the ability to respond quickly to major economic management and national security issues. As a response to changing historical circumstances and the demands placed upon the United States as a world power, policy initiative has shifted from the legislature to the executive, and with this shift, popular support has shifted towards the plebiscitary presidency.[29]

The Supreme Court has also played a key role in creating the presidentially centered government of the modern era. Through a series of cases culminating in the 1937 National Labor Relations Board case, the Supreme Court legitimated the development of the modern presidency by extending the powers of the federal government "over individual citizens."[30] By rejecting the limited federal government role of the traditional era, the Court made it possible for the federal government to embrace new functions and responsibilities, thus altering the development of American federalism and extending the arm of the state directly into citizen's lives.   And it was the office of the presidency, as personified by Franklin Delano Roosevelt, that was best situated to implement the changes reinforced by the Court.[31]

In sum, there are several factors signifying the end of the traditional period and ushering in the modern presidency that are still prevalent in the American political system today.   The change in presidential rhetoric, the role now played by the president as the legislative leader and as the key figure in public policy debates, enlarged staffing afforded the president through the executive office of the presidency, and the president's preoccupation with foreign affairs are major characteristics of the modern presidency.[32]   Underlying all of these features is the development of a personal, plebiscitary presidency that is at the heart of our political system, a presidency that represents a major divergence from the intent of the constitutional framers.

Presidential Scholarship and the Modern Presidency

The Cult of the Presidency

Presidential scholars have contributed to the presidentially centered government and the accompanying citizen expectations of presidential performance that characterize the development of presidential power since Franklin Roosevelt.   The "cult of the presidency," "textbook presidency,"[33] or "savior model"[34] was developed in response to FDR's leadership during the Great Depression, and it prevailed through the presidency of John F. Kennedy.   Underlying this "cult" or model approach is a firm commitment to the presidency as a strong office and to the desirability of this condition for the political system as a whole. Political science texts written during this period concluded approvingly that the presidency was growing larger, while gaining more responsibilities and resources.[35]   The use of laudatory labels, such as "the Wilson years," "the Roosevelt revolution," "the Eisenhower period," and "the Kennedy Camelot years" also fostered the cult of the presidency and reinforced the notion that the president is the key figure in the American political system.   Cronin identifies a number of factors that contributed to the development of the textbook presidency:

1. the rise of the president as the "leader of the free world;"
2. the need for a national symbol of reassurance;
3. the values of liberal pundits and textbook writers;
4. the vast expansion of government coupled with the gradual relinquishment of powers to the president by Congress;
5. the powers for national stability and regime loyalty;
6. the constraints on research and writing about the presidency;
7. the rise of prime-time television coverage of presidential campaigns and presidential performance.[36]

The cult of the presidency has been characterized by three key elements: personalization, enhanced power, and enhanced virtue.[37]

Perhaps no other work contributed more to the development of this approach than Richard Neustadt's *Presidential Power*, which was first published in 1960. Representing a sharp break with the legalistic and constitutional approach that had dominated presidential scholarship up until that time, *Presidential Power* reinforced the notion that strong presidential leadership should be linked to good government. Neustadt eschewed strict legalistic interpretations of presidential power and instead conceived of power in the following way: "'Power' I defined as personal influence on governmental action. This I distinguished sharply—a novel distinction then—from formal powers vested in the Presidency."[38] For Neustadt, the Franklin Delano Roosevelt activist presidency was the ideal model for presidential leadership and the exercise of power. Future presidents, according to Neustadt, should be evaluated on the basis of how well they achieved the standards set by Roosevelt. Like presidential scholars of his time and many since, Neustadt rejected the framers' view that the Congress should be the chief policymaking branch and that the president should be constrained by numerous checks and balances. Instead, Neustadt spoke of "separated institutions sharing powers."[39]

As Neustadt and other scholars embraced a presidentially centered form of government, they failed to recognize the consequences of imposing a new interpretation of the political order on a governmental framework rooted in Madisonian principles. One such consequence has been that as presidents attempt to meet the heightened expectations associated with the modern presidency, they are sometimes driven to assert presidential prerogative powers in ways that threaten both constitutional and democratic principles. The Johnson and Nixon presidencies, in particular, provided empirical evidence to support this concern. In response, presidential scholars embraced a new model for evaluating presidential power: "the imperial presidency."

The Rise of the Imperial Presidency

Concerns about excessive presidential power were articulated in light of Lyndon Johnson's legislative victories in the 1960s, Johnson's and Nixon's decisionmaking in the Vietnam War, the Nixon/Kissinger Cambodian debacle, and the Nixon presidency's disgrace in the wake of Watergate. Presidential scholars began to question whether presidential strength would necessarily lead to the promotion of the general welfare. Scholars spoke of the pathological presidency, reinforcing many of the constitutional framers' fears regarding the consequences of concentrating excessive powers in the executive.

Writing in this vein and responding to presidential excesses in the conduct of the Vietnam War and the Watergate scandal, Arthur Schlesinger, Jr., developed the concept of the "imperial presidency." Schlesinger recognized that the system of checks and balances needed vigorous action by one of the three branches if the stalemate built into the system was to be overcome. Schlesinger believed that the presidency was best equipped to fill this role. Rather than rejecting centralized presidential power per se, he spoke of presidential abuses: "In the last years presidential primacy, so indispensable to the political order, has turned into presidential supremacy. The constitutional Presidency—as events so apparently disparate as the Indochina War and the Watergate affair showed—has become the imperial Presidency and threatens to be the revolutionary Presidency."[40] Schlesinger placed much of the blame for the imperial presidency on presidential excesses in foreign policy, a claim that will be evaluated more fully in Chapter 5. Truman, Kennedy, Johnson, and Nixon interpreted the Constitution to permit the president to commit American combat troops unilaterally, and the prolonged Vietnam War encouraged foreign policy centralization and the use of secrecy.[41] The imperial presidency, or "the presidency as satan model,"[42] can also be applied to the Nixon administration's domestic activities, including wiretapping, the use of impoundments, executive branch reorganization for political purposes, and expansive interpretations of executive privilege.

Schlesinger's analysis is an important contribution to the study of presidential power because it recognizes the limitations imposed by the framers and the potentially negative consequences of the plebiscitary presidency. Yet the imperial presidency model fails to the extent that it, too, accepts presidential governance in a political system grounded in principles and procedures that are inimical to this claim. Chapter 5 argues that Schlesinger's notion needs to be revised to take into account congressional acquiescence in foreign affairs. The 1983 invasion of Grenada, the 1983 bombing of a marine barracks in Lebanon, the 1987

Iran-Contra affair, the 1989 invasion of Panama, and the 1991 Persian Gulf war provide evidence to support this reconceptualization of the imperial presidency.

Congress responded to presidential assertions of power in the domestic and foreign policy arenas by passing the War Powers Resolution of 1973 and by enacting institutional reforms designed to disperse power throughout the House and Senate. These institutional reforms diluted the power of standing committees by providing for a subcommittee bill of rights that guaranteed individual subcommittees more power through independent staffing and funding.[43] In addition, these reforms provided several barriers to presidential legislative leadership including the erosion of seniority, growth in congressional staff, the rise of entrepreneurial members of Congress, the separation of presidential coalitions from congressional coalitions, the weakening of party leadership, and the proliferation of subcommittees.[44]

From the vantage point of the president, these congressional reforms contributed to greater congressional fragmentation and member independence. Presidents now find it increasingly difficult to translate their domestic campaign promises into concrete public policy in light of these reforms. This has led the British journalist Godfrey Hodgson to conclude that "the paradox of congressional power exactly matches the paradox of presidential power. The power of Congress is enormous; it is still not enough to do the things that must be done."[45] In response to the perceived failures and weaknesses of the Ford and Carter eras, presidential scholars revised their models of the presidency once again, this time to bemoan the "impossible presidency."

The Impossible Presidency

The need to recognize institutional limits on presidents' abilities to translate their campaign promises into concrete public policy is a central theme characterizing much of the presidency literature during the 1980s and early 1990s.[46] Scholars have argued that the so-called textbook presidency paints an unrealistic picture of presidential power within the confines of a Madisonian framework of separated powers and checks and balances. Others have said that this unrealistic vision has contributed to the "cult of the presidency,"[47] which is reinforced by the political socialization process and the media, thus leading to the "no-win"[48] or "impossible"[49] presidencies. The notion of a plural executive, whose powers are fragmented throughout the Madisonian system, has grown in popularity among scholars.[50]

Presidential scholars, distressed by the development of the impossible presidency, linked Gerald Ford's and Jimmy Carter's so-called failed presidencies to unrealistic citizen expectations that emanate "from the tensions generated by the office's strong symbolic position in American life and its inability to respond to economic, social, and political forces with any degree of predictable success."[61] The impossible presidency model recognizes that a president's inability to meet public expectations is rooted in the structure of the Madisonian system, a system that provides "constitutional dependence on other political institutions for support,"[62] and in the controversial policy concerns facing presidents who must gain the support of Congress and the American people in a time of increased resource scarcity. The kinds of redistributive questions associated with such issues as energy and environmental concerns, homelessness, education, the budget deficit, and defense spending are guaranteed to elicit hostile responses from various citizen interests; and as the most visible figure in the American political system, the president is most likely to be blamed. The media merely serve to exacerbate the impossible presidency by focusing attention on the first family's daily activities and ignoring other relevant aspects of the American policy process, including the role played by the other two branches of government. Finally, scholars have identified the decline in the role of parties as coalition-building devices. What it takes to get elected is no longer adequate to the task of building the effective governing coalitions needed to break the Madisonian deadlock.[63]

The strength of the impossible presidency model is that it recognizes institutional constraints on presidents' abilities to meet the unrealistic expectations associated with presidential governance. In this sense, it goes much further than the textbook and imperial presidency models in linking the consequences of the constitutional framers' intentions to broader systemic constraints facing the modern presidency today.

Yet the model is not without its weaknesses. It fails to respond to those who point to the policy successes of Roosevelt's New Deal initiatives, Johnson's Great Society, and Reagan's first-year tax and budgetary cut proposals as evidence that great leaders can inspire Congress and the American people to support presidential policy leadership. In addition, like the other models, it also tacitly supports vigorous presidential leadership by lamenting its very absence and proposing structural revisions of the Madisonian framework that will help achieve this goal. These proposals have included, at various times, the following reforms:

1. the team ticket, whereby the president and members of Congress would be elected on the same ballot, thus fostering electoral support for linkage between congress and the president;
2. the Reuss proposal, whereby the President could choose senators or representatives for Cabinet membership without requiring them to vacate their congressional seats;

3. change in the length of terms for House of Representative members from two to four years, thus providing more continuity between the legislature and the executive; and

4. a vote of no-confidence for the president when he has irretrievably lost the confidence of the nation, allowing for his removal through impeachment.[54]

The strength of these measures is that their proposers recognize the futility of expecting presidents to dominate a policy process that was created with procedures built in to check and limit such domination. Unfortunately, such reforms are often proposed without a mature discussion of the barriers to enacting such radical constitutional change in a conservative political system that by its structure and ideology rejects such change. How these barriers might be overcome and what might prompt such constitutional change needs to be considered in greater detail.

The development of the impossible presidency model and accompanying structural reforms has stimulated new debate among presidential scholars regarding whether the modern presidency paradigm should be rejected in light of the changes associated with the Oval Office during the 1980s and early 1990s. Scholars have now begun to speak of the postmodern presidency to signify the changing sources of presidential power as we head into the twenty-first century. Whether the changes in presidential power warrant such treatment is the focus of the following section.

The Viability of the "Postmodern Presidency"

The move from the traditional to the modern presidency was rooted in the presidencies of Theodore Roosevelt and Woodrow Wilson and culminated during the era of Franklin Delano Roosevelt. As we have seen, underlying this shift were changes in presidential rhetoric, presidential leadership of Congress, and the relationship of the federal government to the citizenry as personified by the altered role of the president in the American political system. Have such major changes in the role of the presidency occurred during the past two decades that they indicate the passage of the modern era and the birth of the postmodern presidency?

Two recent works on the presidency make such a claim. In *The Post-Modern Presidency* Ryan Barilleaux contends that the shift from the modern era is rooted in trends and events associated with Watergate and Vietnam. Barilleaux argues that many of the developments associated with the postmodern presidency have existed "throughout the modern period of the office, but it was in their fulfillment that the change occurred."[55] Furthermore, Barilleaux asserts that accompanying the rise of the postmodern presidency is a new political environment characterized by institutional change, individualized politics, fiscal stress, and a major shift in the use of political power by unelected officials in the judiciary and bureaucracy.[56] He concludes that the postmodern presidency is distinguished from the traditional and modern eras by the following features:

1. the revival of presidential prerogative power;
2. governing through public politics;
3. the president's general secretariat;
4. vicarious policymaking;
5. the president as chief whip in Congress;
6. the new vice-presidency.[57]

The Reagan presidency, argues Barilleaux, has helped extend the post-modern presidency by reflecting the above changes. Yet this is hardly a convincing case for the development of the postmodern presidency. For example, Tulis has shown how Woodrow Wilson and Franklin Delano Roosevelt governed through public politics,[58] and various presidents throughout the nineteenth and twentieth centuries have exercised presidential prerogative powers, especially in the foreign policy arena.[59] It is interesting to note, too, that Barilleaux's list of characteristics associated with the postmodern presidency fails to contain any reference to major foreign policy developments. The central problem with Barilleaux's argument is that he fails to emphasize the specific thresholds pointing to significant change that warrant the ushering in of a new presidential era. He does, however, offer a major contribution to the presidency literature with his discussion of the increased role of the president in parallel unilateral policy declarations (PUPD) and arms-control prerogatives.

Richard Rose's version of the postmodern presidency emphasizes different elements than those outlined by Barilleaux. Rose extends Barilleaux's arguments regarding the postmodern presidency by devoting much more attention to the president's changing role in international affairs. For Rose, the defining characteristic of the postmodern presidency can be summarized in a single sentence: "The resources of the White House are not sufficient to meet all of the President's international responsibilities."[60] Identifying Jimmy Carter as the first postmodern president, Rose contends that the Carter presidency first experienced the perils associated with the president's diminished role in the international arena. These perils included global inflation that affected inflation at home, the Soviet invasion of Afghanistan, the rise in oil prices, and the taking of American hostages

in the Middle East.[61]   Like those who advocate the impossible
presidency thesis, Rose blames our presidential selection process for not
preparing candidates for the kind of training needed to govern the
nation should they be elected president: "The biggest problem of the
postmodern President is: What it takes to become President has
nothing to do with what it takes to be President. . . . An even more
troubling prospect must be faced: What it takes to become President
actually makes it more difficult to be a successful postmodern
President."[62]   To be successful, argues Rose, a president must be
willing and trained to bargain with members of Congress within a
system of checks and balances. The use of presidential rhetoric through
"going public" in an effort to campaign for governing support is an
important imperative growing out of the postmodern presidency.
Rose's discussion of public politics is the only area that overlaps
significantly with Barilleaux's conception of the postmodern presidency.
Finally, Rose contends, if presidents are to be successful in the
international arena, they must be willing to bargain "with foreigners on
whose cooperation [they depend] for success in foreign and economic
policy."[63]

    Both Barilleaux's and Rose's analyses of the postmodern presidency
make useful contributions to the study of changing sources of presidential power and the relationship of the electoral process to presidential
governance. Yet the postmodern presidency concept distorts the true
meaning of these shifts. While some of the shifts previously described
were reflected most notably during the Carter and Reagan presidencies,
they do not represent a significant break with the features of the
modern presidency. Instead, they merely reinforce features already
characterizing the modern presidency. Barilleaux and Rose fail to
identify the specific trigger or threshold that indicates a clear transition
to the postmodern era. What are the criteria for moving from one era
to another? This important empirical question is also omitted from their
analyses. If the postmodern presidency concept is to be embraced by
presidential scholars, it must have much stronger grounding in both
theoretical and empirical evidence. In addition, Barilleaux and Rose fail
to develop changes in the central relationship between the office of the
presidency and the citizenry.   In this sense, they overlook a key
development in presidential power first seen during the 1930s and
further in evidence during the presidencies of Nixon and Reagan. The
mature modern presidency is the plebiscitary presidency. This theme
will be developed more fully as Chapter 3 examines the sources of
citizen support for the Oval Office, how presidents have attempted to
use this support in getting elected and ultimately governing the nation,
and what this means for future presidential aspirants. The question of
whether Reagan and Bush have indeed helped to usher in a new era
will be addressed throughout the remainder of this book.

In sum, presidential periodization concepts such as "postmodern" are weakened considerably due to inadequate conceptual development, the lack of a clear threshold or trigger that identifies a shift in presidential epochs, and a failure to recognize that recent trends in the presidency do not represent sufficiently distinct or significant changes to warrant a new presidential era. In addition, certain areas of inquiry, such as the constitutional context for explaining presidential performance and the relationship between the presidency and the citizenry, are afforded short shrift. The plebiscitary presidency, which by its very nature rejects implicit periodization schemes, offers a more useful vehicle for examining changes in presidential power over time.

Critical Reflections on the Plebiscitary Presidency

At the heart of the plebiscitary presidency is the notion that the citizenry looks to the president, as the most visible representative of the federal government, for meeting their needs in the domestic and foreign policy arenas. The plebiscitary presidency does not, however, suggest the development of a new postmodern presidential paradigm. Instead, it suggests a more fully developed modern presidency, one that is confronted with heightened citizen expectations of presidential performance in a time of resource scarcity. In so doing, it implicitly rejects arbitrary attempts at periodization and, as a result, can be a more useful and accurate explanatory construct for detailing changes in presidential power over time. A further strength of the plebiscitary presidency is that it allows presidential scholars to evaluate the structural forces that prevent the fulfillment of a president's campaign promises while recognizing that underlying all of these structural constraints is a lack of fiscal resources.

The new political environment of the 1990s and beyond suggests that presidents will be operating within fiscal constraints and limits on their ability to meet the heightened citizen expectations of presidential performance. Will the constitutional framers' vision of separate institutions sharing powers and their system of checks and balances allow political actors to meet the concerns of all classes in society during a time of increased resource scarcity? This is a compelling question that has generated considerable scholarly discussion.[64] To make matters more difficult, presidents will be forced to uncover new sources of presidential power within the confines of a political framework that was established two hundred years ago specifically to prevent the aggrandizement of power in a single branch of government. How presidents deal with the resource constraints that confront President Bush is a major theme of this book.

The plebiscitary presidency has been a key source of presidential power since 1933. For presidents such as Ford and Carter, however, the heightened expectations associated with the personal, plebiscitary presidency have also led to citizen unhappiness and characterizations of presidential failure. The Carter presidency, in particular, reinforced elements of the plebiscitary presidency. As a "trustee" president, Jimmy Carter reinforced the notion that as the elected representative of all the people, "the president must act as the counterforce to special interests" and provide the leadership necessary in setting the policy agenda and introducing "comprehensive policy proposals."[65] Charles Jones makes a persuasive case that Carter's vision of the trustee presidency was anathema to a Congress that had just passed a series of reforms designed to tame the imperial Nixon presidency. When Carter tried to introduce unpopular energy conservation policies and cut back "unnecessary dams and water projects" because they represented the "worst examples of the pork-barrel,"[66] he challenged Congress and the American people to reject politics as usual. In this sense, he was displaying a style of presidential leadership unseen in recent years, one that reinforced the plebiscitary presidency while at the same time challenging some of the assumptions on which it is based. Unlike his immediate predecessors and successors, Carter at least tried to heighten the level of dialogue around resource scarcity concerns. He soon learned, however, that his unwillingness to cultivate congressional support for his policies and his call for a shared sacrifice on the part of the American people undermined the plebiscitary foundations of the modern presidency. His 1980 presidential challenger understood Carter's problems quite well and was determined not to repeat them. Ronald Reagan's campaign and governing strategies accepted and extended the plebiscitary presidency. This helps to account for his victories in both 1980 and 1984.

How Ronald Reagan uncovered new sources of presidential power rooted in the personal, plebiscitary presidency is the focus of the following chapter. Chapter 3 will outline Reagan's use of a values strategy and his effective manipulation of the media. It will examine his governing strategies, including the rebirth of the administrative presidency and presidential secrecy and deception in foreign policy. The goal is to examine changing sources of presidential power as presidents of the modern era recognize that the Madisonian framework of checks and balances and shared powers prohibits the kinds of sustained presidential policy responses required by the plebiscitary presidency. In the absence of clearly defined and strong constitutional leadership powers, presidents must uncover prerogative and informal powers to meet the imperatives of the personal, plebiscitary presidency. It is to the sources of these powers that we now turn.

Notes

1. Theodore J. Lowi, *The Personal President* (Ithaca: Cornell University Press, 1985), p. 100.

2. See Lowi, 1985, and Theodore J. Lowi, "An Aligning Election: A Presidential Plebiscite," in Michael Nelson, ed., *The Elections of 1984* (Washington, D.C.: Congressional Quarterly Press, 1985), p. 288.

3. See Amitai Etzioni, "Today We Elect a President-Monarch," *New York Times* November 8, 1988, p. A23.

4. Seligman and Covington, 1989, p. 94.

5. Fred I. Greenstein, "Nine Presidents: In Search of a Modern Presidency," in Fred I. Greenstein, ed., *Leadership in the Modern Presidency* (Cambridge, Massachusetts: Harvard University Press, 1988), p. 298.

6. Richard Rose, *The Postmodern President: The White House Meets the World* (Chatham, New Jersey: Chatham House, 1989), p. 21.

7. Rose, 1989, p. 20.

8. Arthur Schlesinger, Jr., *The Imperial Presidency* (Boston: Houghton Mifflin, 1973), p. viii.

9. Rose, 1989, p. 21.

10. Jeffrey K. Tulis, *The Rhetorical Presidency* (Princeton, New Jersey: Princeton University Press, 1987), p. 87.

11. Lowi, 1985, p. 20.

12. Tulis, 1987, p. 173.

13. Gary W. King and Lyn Ragsdale, *The Elusive Executive: Discovering Statistical Patterns in the Presidency* (Washington, D.C.:   Congressional Quarterly Press, 1988), p. 26.

14. Tulis, 1987, p. 138.

15. See William E. Leuchtenburg, *In the Shadow of FDR* (Ithaca: Cornell University Press, 1983).

16. See Seligman and Covington, 1989, pp. 33-35, for the source material that serves as the basis for this discussion of the progressive movement.

17. Seligman and Covington, 1989, p. 41.

18. Fred I. Greenstein, "Nine Presidents In Search of a Modern Presidency," in Fred I. Greenstein, ed., *Leadership in the Modern Presidency* (Cambridge, Massachusetts: Harvard University Press, 1988), p. 298.

19. William E. Leuchtenburg, "Franklin D. Roosevelt: The First Modern President," in Fred I. Greenstein, ed., *Leadership in the Modern Presidency* (Cambridge, Massachusetts: Harvard University Press, 1988), p. 11.

20. During his first hundred days, Franklin Roosevelt pushed Congress to accept an impressive program of legislation, including emergency banking legislation, legislation creating a national agricultural policy, and legislation establishing the Federal Emergency Relief Act, the National Industrial Recovery Act, and the Tennessee Valley Authority. The second hundred days of Roosevelt's tenure witnessed the passage of several key New Deal measures, including a major tax reform bill, the Social Security Act, and the

Wagner Labor Relations Act. For a thoughtful discussion of these legislative accomplishments within the context of the development of the modern presidency, see David Mervin, "The President and Congress," in Malcolm Shaw, ed., *The Modern Presidency: From Roosevelt to Reagan* (New York: Harper and Row, 1987), p. 88.

21. Hugh Heclo, "Introduction: The Presidential Illusion," in Hugh Heclo and Lester M. Salamon, eds., *The Illusion of Presidential Government* (Boulder, Colorado: Westview Press, 1981), p. 2.

22. Michael Nelson, "Evaluating the Presidency," in Michael Nelson, ed., *The Presidency and the Political System*, 2nd ed. (Washington, D.C.: Congressional Quarterly Press, 1988), p. 20. World War II also undoubtedly contributed to the institutionalization of presidential power, and the postwar emphasis on national security sustained it.

23. Harold M. Barger, *The Impossible Presidency: Illusions and Realities of Presidential Power* (Chicago: Scott Foresman, 1984), p. 18.

24. Lowi, 1985, pp. 61-62.

25. Lowi, 1985, p. 96.

26. Thomas E. Cronin, *The State of the Presidency*, 2nd ed. (Boston: Little, Brown, 1980), p. 91.

27. Robinson, 1987, pp. 112-113.

28. See Lowi, 1985, and Theodore J. Lowi, *The End of Liberalism: The Second Republic of the United States*, 2nd ed. (New York: Norton, 1979).

29. Robinson, 1987, pp. 115-117.

30. Lowi, 1985, p. 48.

31. I am indebted to Theodore Lowi for his insightful analysis of the role of the Supreme Court in reinforcing the developments associated with the move from the traditional to the modern eras. For Lowi's analysis, which serves as the basis of my own discussion, see Lowi, 1985, Chapter 3.

32. Malcolm Shaw, "The Traditional and Modern Presidencies," in Malcolm Shaw, ed., *The Modern Presidency: From Roosevelt to Reagan* (New York: Harper and Row, 1987), p. 294.

33. See Thomas E. Cronin, *The State of the Presidency*, 2nd ed. (Boston: Little, Brown, 1980), p. 76.

34. See Nelson, 1988, p. 7.

35. Cronin, 1980, p. 79.

36. Cronin, 1980, p. 85.

37. Hinckley, 1985, p. 38.

38. Richard E. Neustadt, *Presidential Power: The Politics of Leadership from FDR to Carter* (New York: John Wiley and Sons, 1980), p. xi.

39. Neustadt, 1980, p. 26.

40. Arthur Schlesinger, Jr., *The Imperial Presidency* (Boston: Houghton Mifflin, 1973), p. viii.

41. Schlesinger, 1973, p. 208.

42. Nelson, 1988, p. 10.

43. Harold M. Barger, *The Impossible Presidency: Illusions and Realities of Presidential Power* (Glenview, Illinois: Scott Foresman, 1984), p. 134.

44. This discussion is based on Seligman and Covington's (1989) excellent overview of emerging barriers to presidential legislative leadership, pp. 78-84.

45. Godfrey Hodgson, *All Things to All Men* (New York: Simon and Schuster, 1980), p. 158.

46. See Barger, 1984; Cronin, 1980; Hinckley, 1985; and Paul C. Light, *The President's Agenda: With Notes on Ronald Reagan* (Baltimore: Johns Hopkins University Press, 1983).

47. See Hinckley, 1985.

48. See Light, 1983.

49. See Barger, 1984.

50. Gary King and Lyn Ragsdale, *The Elusive Executive: Discovering Statistical Patterns in the Presidency* (Washington, D.C.: Congressional Quarterly Press, 1988).

51. Barger, 1984, p. 13.

52. Nelson, 1988, p. 9.

53. For thoughtful discussions of the decline in the role of political parties as governing coalition-building devices, see James MacGregor Burns, *The Power to Lead: The Crisis of the American Presidency* (New York: Simon and Schuster, 1984) and Seligman and Covington, 1989.

54. See Burns, 1984, p. 237; James L. Sundquist, *Constitutional Reform & Effective Government* (Washington, D.C.: Brookings Institution, 1986); and Robinson, 1987 for thoughtful discussions of these and other reforms.

55. Ryan J. Barilleaux, *The Post-Modern Presidency* (New York: Praeger, 1988), p. 44.

56. Barilleaux, 1988, p. 61.

57. Barilleaux, 1988, p. 8.

58. Tulis, 1987.

59. See Schlesinger, Jr., 1973, and William Shawcross, *Sideshow: Kissinger, Nixon and the Destruction of Cambodia* (New York: Touchstone, 1989).

60. Rose, 1989, p. 25.

61. Rose, 1989, pp. 25-26.

62. Rose, 1989, p. 6.

63. Rose, 1989, p. 8.

64. See Burns, 1984; Herson, 1984; and Sundquist, 1986.

65. Charles O. Jones, *The Trusteeship Presidency* (Baton Rouge: Louisiana State University Press, 1988), p. 6.

66. Jones, 1988, p. 143.

3

Public Politics and the Use of Values in the Reagan and Bush Eras

"We're going forward with values that have never failed us when we lived up to them: dignity of work, love for family and neighborhood, faith in God, belief in peace through strength, and a commitment to protect the freedom which is our legacy as Americans."[1] This clear statement espousing the values associated with American exceptionalism was vintage Ronald Reagan. Although he made this promise on the 1984 campaign trail, he articulated the same values approach as a presidential aspirant in 1979 as well as during his two terms as president. What distinguished Reagan's own use of the values approach from the approaches of previous occupants of the Oval Office was his effective use of the mass media, especially television, to communicate his shared vision for a better America. In the absence of the cohesive political parties that are needed not only to get elected but also to build governing coalitions, Reagan created his own governing coalition rooted in the politics of shared values. His ability to fashion this new governing coalition represents an extension of presidential prerogative power that has been available to presidents since Roosevelt's fireside radio chats in the 1930s. By appealing to the values associated with American exceptionalism through "going public," Reagan helped to more fully develop the plebiscitary presidency.

American exceptionalism is the belief that the United States "is inevitably destined for economic and political greatness."[2] It is also rooted in the conviction that the values accepted by the constitutional framers are still relevant today and will continue to be relevant in the future. At the core of the plebiscitary presidency is the president's symbolic role as the leader of the nation and chief proponent of the values associated with American exceptionalism. As numerous scholars have suggested, the United States is one of the few nations that requires its chief executive to serve both as the chief executive and as the symbolic, ceremonial head of state.[3] The view that the presidency is best able to represent the national interest is accepted by occupants of the Oval Office and reinforced by public opinion.[4] If presidents are to be successful in fulfilling these demands, they must articulate clearly and convincingly the classical liberal values of individualism and freedom, equality of opportunity, hard work, religiosity, and free enterprise values that underlie American exceptionalism.

This chapter argues that Ronald Reagan was particularly adept in fulfilling the requirements associated with the modern, plebiscitary presidency. His outgoing January 1989 public opinion ratings (see Figure 3.1) provide empirical evidence to support this claim and leave a difficult standard for future presidents to achieve.

Yet while Reagan's values approach allowed him to cement his personal popularity, it did not enable him to achieve many of the conservative policy goals articulated in his two presidential campaigns. Reagan did well in persuading Congress to support many of his domestic policies during his extended honeymoon period but failed to sustain policy success over the duration of his presidency. A president's use of the rhetorical presidency cannot be a long-term substitute for the governing coalitions rooted in coherent political parties that allow presidents to translate campaign promises into concrete public policy. To be sure, an emphasis on symbolism and values reinforces the heightened citizen expectations of presidential performance associated with the plebiscitary presidency. This trend is disturbing, however, to the extent that presidents must operate within a Madisonian policy process established to check and balance presidential leadership. The upshot is that President Bush and future occupants of the Oval Office may find it increasingly difficult to meet citizen expectations by merely "going public" and communicating a shared vision of values in a time of fiscal austerity; and a failure to meet these expectations will raise difficult redistributive questions about the capability of the political system to respond to the concerns of all classes in society. In his presidential campaign and his first term, George Bush has already recognized the importance of appealing to shared American values and using the media to cement his popularity (see Figure 3.2).

Whether this popularity can be translated into domestic policy success and long-term support in Congress and with the American people remains to be seen. The lack of a policy mandate and the thinness of his campaign message has also undermined the Bush administration's domestic policy efforts. Gary Trudeau captured the

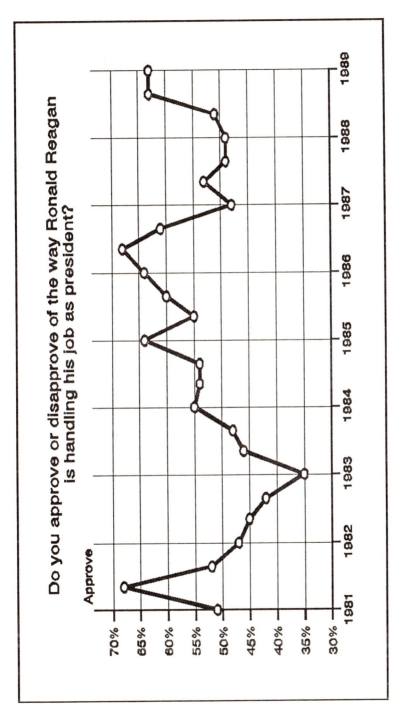

FIGURE 3.1 A Profile of Reagan's Presidential Popularity, 1981-1989. Sources: *Gallup Opinion Index; Gallup Report; Gallup Poll Monthly.*

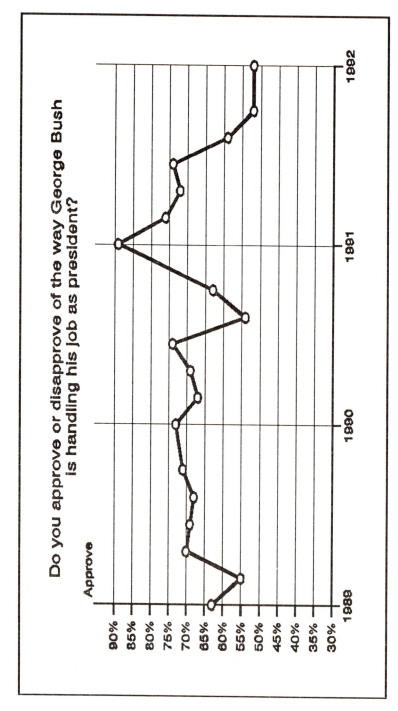

FIGURE 3.2 A Profile of Bush's Presidential Popularity 1989-1991. Sources: *Gallup Opinion Index; Gallup Report; Gallup Poll Monthly.*

essence of Bush's problem just before his inaugural: "So far today, I've said the Pledge and I haven't joined the ACLU and I haven't furloughed any murderers. I've delivered on my entire mandate, and it isn't even lunch yet."[5] George Bush and his advisors have worked to build on the presidency's exalted standing in the minds of the American people by reinforcing symbols that proved successful during the 1988 campaign.

There is little doubt that for many citizens, the president is in the best position to promote the values associated with the "exceptional American experience." Lofty expectations for the presidency are deeply rooted in the American political culture and its fervent belief in American exceptionalism. The consequences of these heightened expectations of presidential performance, the forces perpetuating these unrealistic images, and the implications for sources of presidential power in the modern era are topics to which we now turn.

Political Socialization and the American Presidency

American attitudes and beliefs regarding the role of the presidency in the political system are the basis for the gap between what Americans expect their presidents to achieve and what presidents are capable of achieving in a Madisonian framework of checks and balances and shared powers. Political socialization is the process by which these attitudes and beliefs regarding the political system are acquired. As discussed in Chapter 2, government and history texts have provided an idealized view of the role of the presidency in the American political system. The political socialization process paints a distorted picture of presidential power and thus contributes to the miseducation of the citizenry. By emphasizing the symbolic and leadership roles that presidents play, educators and the media convey a false impression of the president's role in the American political system and thus heighten citizen expectations of presidential performance. Research findings on the political socialization process offer evidence to support these claims.

Studies of political socialization and the American presidency[6] reveal that the contemporary president is expected to be strong, assertive, competent, virtuous, and, above all, a savior.[7] Children are inculcated with these beliefs at an early age. White, middle-class children view the American political system in positive and highly idealized terms. The president is regarded as a benevolent, God-like leader who can be trusted and respected as a key authority figure, much like a child's father. In their studies of children in Chicago and comparative work in other American cities, Hess and Torney provide empirical evidence to support these conclusions:

> Young children relate to the president as they do to figures they know
> personally, expressing strong emotional attachment to him and
> expecting protection from him. They believe that the president is
> intimately involved not only in momentous decisions concerning the
> fate of the country but also in more mundane decisions that affect them
> and their neighborhood. . . . A strong sense of trust is evident in their
> responses; they think that the president is personally responsive to
> children's wishes and believe that they could even go to the White
> House and talk to him.[8]

At an early age, then, children develop the personalized respect for the
presidency that characterizes their attitudes as adults. This suggests that
if a more realistic citizen understanding of presidential power is to be
achieved, it must be accomplished early in a child's education.

It is interesting to note that children's attitudes regarding the
presidency may be affected by class. Studies have shown that children
from poor backgrounds have less idealistic visions of government and
tend to be more critical of the presidency. This conclusion pertains both
to minority group members as well as to rural Appalachian children.[9]
These children, then, may have a more realistic vision of presidential
power than the majority of children who are socialized into the middle-
class American values associated with American exceptionalism.

As children grow older, they may develop greater abilities to
evaluate individual presidents critically; but research has shown that
most teenagers still have great respect for the presidency. This can be
attributed to the glowing image of presidential power portrayed in high
school and college texts.

Like children, adults view the president as the central symbol of
government and often blindly give their support to the occupant of the
Oval Office as well as to the presidency itself. Greenstein's empirical
research has found that adults view the president as the most important
actor in the American political system.[10] Other studies have found that
citizens have such reverence and respect for the presidency that they
believe in supporting a president's actions, even if the actions might be
wrong.[11] Roberta Sigel's 1966 study of personal support for the
presidency uncovered disturbing findings about citizens' views on
presidential power. When asked, "Once the president has made up his
mind on a matter of public policy, do any of the people below have a
right to try to make him change his mind?" 71 percent concluded that
the cabinet did, 69 percent believed that Congress did, and 67 percent
said the American people had the right to do so.[12] These findings
suggest that the attitudes regarding the primacy of the American
political system, first developed as children, are prevalent in adults as

well. The findings also raise serious questions about what citizens are being taught regarding presidential power and the implications of the political socialization process for presidential governance, democratic accountability, and the development of citizenship.

No modern president can expect to succeed without the support of the public. Yet this support must be grounded in a firm rejection of the unrealistic textbook-presidency notion of presidential power. While it is in their interests to foster more realistic citizen expectations of actual presidential powers, most presidents instead use the symbolic trappings of the office to create the illusion of presidential governance. In this sense, they merely reinforce the political socialization process. When they have attempted to communicate a more realistic sense of constraints on presidential power, their efforts, as in Jimmy Carter's case, have often been met with ridicule and judgments of failure.

The Reagan years offer a sharp departure from the Carter approach to governance. Whereas Jimmy Carter often spoke of limits, Ronald Reagan exalted the possibilities associated with the American Dream and the Protestant work ethic. As both a presidential candidate and occupant of the Oval Office, Reagan articulated a vision of shared American values and uncovered a new source of presidential power rooted in the effective use of media technology. This new power source has opened up an avenue of governance for future occupants of the Oval Office that recognizes the inability of presidents to appeal solely to party label for building governing coalitions and that instead emphasizes a shared commitment to common core values. Ronald Reagan, therefore, has extended the political socialization process even further by relying on the values associated with American exceptionalism and by embracing an activist presidential role in extending such values. In this way, he has contributed to the development of the electronic plebiscitary presidency.[13]

A Values Approach to Governance

Studies of Reagan's campaign and governing rhetoric suggest that he had a firm commitment to the underlying values associated with American exceptionalism. His speeches and public pronouncements resonated with the principles of family, freedom, equality of opportunity, localism, limited government, and free enterprise.[14] Much of this commitment to "old values" derived from his "life and career, which have been shaped by traditional ideas about freedom, hard work, and morality."[15]

Having established these themes during his presidential campaigns, Reagan and his aides set the necessary foundation for a governing strategy. Aldrich and Weko argue that "campaign strategy not only helps to frame the choices of the electorate, it also helps to frame the victor's postelection political agenda."[16] Reagan's campaign strategists recognized this important rule of American politics and made sure that their candidate continued to employ powerful political symbols while articulating the possibilities of the American Dream.

Reagan's strategy was in clear conflict with the strategies used by his opponents in the 1980 and 1984 presidential elections. While Jimmy Carter and Walter Mondale also appealed to shared American values, they did not match Reagan in articulating an optimistic vision of the future. Their inability to do so likely contributed to voter antipathy toward their candidacies. It is important to note, however, that perhaps Carter and Mondale had a more realistic vision of the future as they recognized the limitations associated with fiscal austerity, budgetary deficits, and energy resource constraints. Unlike Reagan, they tried to impart this more realistic vision to the citizenry, thus challenging a key element of the plebiscitary presidency.

Reagan's own early legislative success has been attributed to his outstanding political and communication skills, the appeal of his antigovernment message during the 1980 campaign (which established a solid foundation for governance), and his ability to give the American people a "sense of return" to their values.[17] All of these factors played a big role in the early success of his legislative agenda. Reagan himself recognized that his background as an actor was helpful in communicating with the American people. Late in his second term, he told ABC's David Brinkley: "There have been times in this office when I've wondered how you could do the job if you hadn't been an actor."[18] Reagan also benefitted from the normal presidential honeymoon period, which was extended after John Hinkley's assassination attempt. Michael Nelson argues persuasively that "the public's emotional attachment to the presidency has implications of its own for strong leadership. The honeymoon that each new president enjoys with the people at the start of his term is, in a sense, an affirmation of faith in the office."[19]

George Bush has also recognized that a values approach to the presidential campaign is a powerful tool for getting elected. Appeals to patriotism, family, and freedom punctuated his campaign rhetoric at the expense of clearly articulating his policy positions on the issues of the day, including the deficit, Star Wars spending, education, and health care. Unlike Reagan, who articulated clear policy positions grounded in shared values, Bush faces the difficult task of building policy coalitions from a divided legislature in the absence of his own commitment to a visible policy agenda. In addition, Bush faces the challenge of following a tremendously popular president of his own party, a president who left a bloated federal deficit that constrained Bush's policy options. A more cynical and accurate explanation for Bush's approach to domestic policy is that his claim to be the "education" and "environmental" president was mere campaign rhetoric, and the deficit served as a convenient rationale for the Bush administration's rejection of increased federal spending in the social policy arena. Finally, Bush has had to confront the difficult political problem of "how to present himself as the legitimate heir to Ronald Reagan and simultaneously establish himself as his own man and maintain the Republican coalition."[20]

As he has demonstrated in his first term, President Bush will likely continue to frame his presidential speeches within the context of shared American values in the absence of a clear governing coalition. Like Reagan, Bush has turned to television, the most important tool of the electronic plebiscitary presidency, for building public support in the absence of coherent political parties. But as will be seen in the next section, he uses television in a very different way than his predecessor.

The Media and the Plebiscitary Presidency

As discussed in Chapter 2, the development of the rhetorical presidency represents a sharp break from the intentions of the constitutional framers as well as a new source of prerogative power available to presidents in the modern age. The Reagan presidency made its own contributions to the development of the rhetorical presidency and set a new standard for occupants of the Oval Office to follow in manipulating the media to promote public support. William Muir contends that Ronald Reagan "set out to define a philosophy of freedom, to distinguish it from a philosophy of equality, and to plant it in the soul of the nation."[21] Reagan's use of carefully scripted presidential appearances via television and radio allowed him to establish his values message in a powerful and convincing way. In many ways, the media remain an important factor in the mismatch between the image of the president and the reality of meeting heightened expectations in a Madisonian policy process characterized by checks and balances and shared powers. The Reagan experience does reveal, however, how presidents can use television and direct media appeals to retain power, build public support, and influence policy by communicating directly to the American people. These techniques are important developments in the plebiscitary presidency that has matured in the absence of coherent political parties. In addition to his use of a values approach, Reagan's use of the media as a new source of presidential power has been characterized by the strategies of "going public," adept use of public relations and media manipulation, and avoidance of spontaneous media experiences that play to the president's weaknesses.

"Going Public" as a Political Strategy

The public's value to the president is derived from the strength it offers in persuading other political actors to support presidential policies and appointments. With popular support, presidents may have a better chance of persuading Congress, the bureaucracy, interest groups, and the media to support presidential initiatives.[22] This important point explains why presidents in the modern era have attempted to garner public support throughout their tenures in office. In sum, public support has been a crucial determinant of presidential power.

With the development of television, presidents have extended the practice legitimated by FDR in his "fireside chats." In times of trouble or crisis, presidents turn to the medium of television to communicate directly with the American people. Examples of this include John F. Kennedy's response to the Bay of Pigs fiasco, Johnson's and Nixon's handling of the Vietnam War, Nixon's response to Watergate, Ford's announcement and defense of Nixon's pardon, Carter's response to the energy crisis, and Reagan's handling of the Iran-Contra affair. Samuel Kernell has labeled this rhetorical strategy "going public" and defines it as "a class of activities in which presidents engage as they promote themselves and their policies before the American public." Examples of "going public" include a primetime address to the nation, a televised press conference, a speech before a business convention, and a presidential trip to China. All of these media events rely on television to communicate a message to the American people. In addition, "they are intended principally to place the president and his message before the American people in a way that enhances his chances of success in Washington."[23] "Going public," then, is an extension and intensification of the rhetorical presidency in the age of television.

Throughout his two terms, Ronald Reagan relied on "going public" activities to build public support for his presidency and for potentially unpopular policies. He did so in an effort to rally public support and direct citizen pressure toward Congress on behalf of his tax cut and budgetary cut proposals as well as his aid to the Nicaraguan Contras. Reagan's own background and training as an actor enhanced his ability to convey a message that had been carefully crafted by his speechwriters and media handlers. Yet his own rhetorical prowess was not enough to avoid significant domestic and foreign policy defeats at the hands of Congress after his first two years in office. What this suggests is that the limits of "going public" and the rhetorical presidency are rooted in a Madisonian framework that was created to prevent the sort of plebiscitary leadership that characterizes the relationship of the citizenry to the office of the presidency today. Tulis argues that excessive reliance on the rhetorical presidency may actually impede governance because the kind of bargaining needed to move Congress to action in the fragmented policy process is often eliminated when presidents "go public."[24]

Reagan did engage in a dual strategy by attempting to balance the more traditional legislative bargaining with "going public."[25] Yet in many cases, such as his Star Wars fight, he emphasized the latter at the expense of negotiating directly with Congress. His experience suggests that presidents cannot rely solely on "going public" as a means for prompting congressional action. A president who wishes to build congressional bipartisan coalitions along with the necessary public support will likely pursue a dual strategy.

Public Relations, Media Manipulation, and the "Teflon Presidency"

While Reagan maintained solid public support in the form of high approval ratings, he did not build public support for many of his policies, including aid to the Nicaraguan Contras, Star Wars, opposition to abortion, and a variety of program budgetary cutbacks.[26] Because his own policy agenda was far more conservative than public sentiment, Reagan and his advisors recognized the need for favorable press treatment. As a part of their media strategy, they attempted to control the policy agenda and establish the context for debate. They did so by creating a Nixon-like public relations apparatus that gave David Gergen (in Reagan's first term) and Michael Deaver the responsibility to handle Reagan's press relationships. Reagan's opportunities to go public were tightly controlled and choreographed to insure that the president appeared as favorably as possible on the evening news. The same kind of approach is used by presidential candidates in the primary and general elections. This suggests that in a very important way television largely dictates not only who is elected as President but how the public responds to that individual once the president arrives in Washington. Walter Mondale lamented the crucial role played by television as he evaluated his 1984 presidential defeat the day after the election: "Modern politics requires television. I've never really warmed up to television. And, in fairness to television, it never warmed up to me. . . . I don't believe it's possible anymore to run for president without the capacity to build confidence and communications every night. It's got to be done that way."[27] Mondale recognized that television is a distinguishing feature of the mature modern presidency and one that will likely continue in the absence of coherent political parties.

In his study of how the press treated the Reagan era, Mark Hertsgaard offers this analysis of Reagan's public relations model: "The Reagan model worked so well that the relationship between the White House and the press will never be the same again. Long after Ronald Reagan left the White House, the model of news management introduced during his tenure will remain behind, shaping press coverage and therefore public perception."[28] The success of the Reagan public relations team can be attributed to several factors. First, the media thrives on covering the symbolic trappings associated with the White House. When former President Jimmy Carter held several town meetings across the United States in an effort to project his image as a president of the people, the media covered the events in detail. They emphasized his overnight stay with selected families; photographs and television footage showed Carter at the breakfast table, talking casually with his hosts.[29] Reagan also benefitted from such media coverage throughout his eight years in office. Second, the media tends to emphasize personality over substance, and Reagan's friendly and engaging personality held the press largely at bay until the Iran-Contra affair. This led Representative Patricia Schroeder (D-Colorado) to deem the Reagan presidency the "teflon presidency" because blame never stuck to Ronald Reagan, even after the Beirut bombing that killed 241 marines.[30] Finally, as numerous scholars have pointed out, the presidential mystique often overwhelms the reporting industry. Grossman and Kumar argue that the overexposure of the White House leads to a heightened public sense that presidential accomplishments are great and setbacks cataclysmic.[31] This means that the public is provided an unrealistic understanding of presidential power in the face of systemic constraints. Gergen and Deaver used this unrealistic reporting to their advantage. They attempted to exercise as much control as possible over how Reagan's policies were portrayed in the press, for they realized that the press is where the citizenry gains most of its information regarding politics. By controlling and releasing information in a timely fashion to enhance favorable press coverage, the Reagan White House set a new standard for manipulating the press and exercising a new source of presidential power.

Damage Control: The Presidential Press Conference

The Reagan team also attempted to use the presidential press conference as a vehicle for showcasing presidential leadership and manipulating the press. A number of changes were introduced to display the president in charge:

> The president's staff made it clear at the beginning of the first term that Mr. Reagan would recognize only those reporters whose hands were raised, and would not respond to shouts of his name as his predecessors had done. Journalists were also required to remain seated when not actually called upon by the president, whereas previous press conferences had been conducted with reporters on their feet. The more controlled atmosphere of a Reagan press conference contributed to the appearance of a president in charge of his office.[32]

Unlike previous presidents such as Kennedy and Carter, Reagan performed poorly in the spontaneous atmosphere of the press conference. He often seemed unsure himself, made embarrassing factual errors, and appeared unaware of the basic elements of his own policies. More than once, press secretaries Larry Speakes or Marlin Fitzwater were drafted to engage in "spin control" in an effort to clarify the president's press conference misstatements and to forestall the accompanying negative press coverage. Reagan's media advisors soon recognized that his poor performance in unscripted press conference settings would undermine the image of presidential control and leadership that they had labored mightily to convey. As a result, few press conferences were scheduled after Reagan's first year. In the end, Reagan held fewer press conferences than any president in this century (see Table 3.1).

The American public, then, only had a chance to see the president in carefully scripted settings, such as photo opportunities on the evening news or the front page of the daily paper, and when he gave formal speeches that had been largely crafted by his aides. The president had thus become more isolated, yet he still maintained the support of a large majority of the American people. In this sense, Reagan's media advisors had uncovered a source of presidential power available to all occupants of the Oval Office. Moreover, they had manipulated the media to develop the plebiscitary presidency to its fullest potential and to enhance public support for Ronald Reagan and his proposed policies.

George Bush has also used the media to bolster his public opinion standing. Unlike Ronald Reagan, he has relied on the presidential news conference as the crucial element in his media strategy. Bush held more press conferences in his first seventeen months in office than Reagan held in eight years.[33] At one point, reporters even complained of "too much access" when they had little to discuss with him at an April 1990

TABLE 3.1 Frequency of Presidential News Conferences, 1929-1992.

Presidents	Monthly Average	Total
Hoover (1929-1933)	5.6	268
Roosevelt (1933-1945)	6.9	998
Truman (1945-1953)	3.4	334
Eisenhower (1953-1961)	2.0	193
Kennedy (1961-1963)	2.9	64
Johnson (1963-1969)	2.2	135
Nixon (1969-1974)	0.5	37
Ford (1974-1977)	1.3	39
Carter (1977-1981)	0.8	59
Reagan (1981-1988)	0.5	42
Bush (1989-1992)	4.7	121

Source: Samuel Kernell, *Going Public* (Washington, D.C.: Congressional Quarterly Press, 1986), p. 69; Thomas Dye and Harman Ziegler, *American Politics in the Media Age*, 3rd ed. (Belmont, California: Brooks Cole, 1989), p. 247; and *Weekly Compilation of Presidential Documents* (Washington, D.C.: Office of the Federal Register, National Archives and Records Service, General Services Administration).

photo opportunity. His approach has paid off, however. The same press that had criticized him during the 1988 campaign adopted a much more positive tone when the public was subjected to story after story of Bush's "informal social style and his athletic prowess."[34] As George Edwards points out, "the result is that the press corps generally likes and respects Bush."[35]

While Bush has embraced presidential press conferences and informal gatherings as his central media strategy, he has eschewed the primetime television address to the nation that was a hallmark of the Reagan presidency. Unlike his predecessor, he is clearly uncomfortable in such settings. Party officials and communication experts argue that Bush fails to impress in carefully scripted televised settings because of his communication style. Democratic media consultant Robert D. Squier contends that Bush "sounds like he comes from the planet Prep. He sounds different from all of us. He has a way of communicating that never sounds quite right." Robert Goodman, who produced Bush campaign commercials in 1980, said that "he is overly enthusiastic. He doesn't give an image of sobriety. I don't think George understands theater; instead of being a salesman, he has to inspire."[36] In a major primetime speech to the nation outlining his War on Drugs, Bush held up a bag of crack that he claimed had been purchased in Lafayette Park, across from the White House. The drug buy was a phony and "the president was upstaged by the prop."[37] For days after the speech, the focus was not on the administration's War on Drugs, but on the hoax that the president had tried to sell to the American people. After this embarrassing experience, it is no surprise that President Bush has tried to minimize the number of his televised addresses to the nation. Yet he has also proved that a president does not have to be a master of the television address to be a popular president.

One important lesson of the Bush administration's performance thus far is that "you do not have to be an actor to obtain public support."[38] He has done particularly in extending his 1988 campaign emphasis on shared American values to his efforts in garnering public support. But this strategy has not worked in inspiring Congress to tackle the domestic policy concerns on the national agenda today. Of course, Bush himself has made it clear that he has more interest in foreign affairs than domestic issues, which is a major reason for his lack of success in the domestic arena. At the same time, he has been forced to frame a governing coalition within the broader context of a Congress that is increasingly characterized by a decline in the importance of political parties and by greater policy fragmentation.

The Decline of Political Parties

As the modern, plebiscitary presidency has matured, political parties have become less important vehicles for providing the governing coalitions that presidents need to translate campaign promises into concrete public policy. As a result, presidents must now build their own coalitions once they assume office. The media have replaced political parties as the principal mechanism available to presidents in the modern era for building electoral and governing coalitions.[39]

The decline in the role of political parties can be attributed to several factors: an increase in the number of independents (see Table 3.2); a rise in split-ticket voting; and a concomitant increase in split electoral outcomes (see Table 3.3). All of these factors can lead to a more independent Congress. Although these trends have been well documented by students of political parties and voting behavior,[40] their consequences for the president need to be more closely studied.

One consequence of the declining role of political parties is that a president must continue to campaign for support even after the general

TABLE 3.2 Partisanship Trends in the Electorate

	1952	1954	1956	1958	1960	1962	1964	1966	1968	1970	1972	1974	1976	1978	1980	1982	1984	1986
Democrats	47	47	44	47	46	46	51	45	45	43	40	38	40	39	39	44	37	41
Independents	22	22	24	19	23	22	23	28	30	31	35	37	36	38	35	30	35	34
Republicans	27	27	29	29	27	28	24	25	24	25	23	22	23	21	24	24	28	26

	1952-1968	1970-1978	1980-1986
Democrats			
Mean	46.4	40.0	40.2
Standard deviation	1.9	1.7	2.6
Independents			
Mean	23.7	35.4	33.5
Standard deviation	3.2	2.4	2.1
Republicans			
Mean	26.7	22.8	25.5
Standard deviation	1.8	1.3	1.6

Source: Lester G. Seligman and Cary R. Covington, *The Coalitional Presidency* (Chicago: Richard Irwin, 1989). Copyright © 1989 by Wadsworth, Inc. Reprinted by permission of Wadsworth Publishing Co., Belmont, California. Data derived from the Center for Political Studies, University of Michigan.

TABLE 3.3 Districts Carried by Congressional and Presidential Candidates of Different Parties, 1900-1984.

Year	Percentage
1900	3
1908	7
1916	11
1924	12
1932	14
1940	15
1948	21
1952	19
1956	30
1960	26
1964	33
1968	32
1972	44
1976	29
1980	34
1984	44

Source: Morris P. Fiorina, "The Presidency and Congress, " in Michael Nelson, ed., *The Presidency and The Political System*, 2nd ed. (Washington, D.C.: Congressional Quarterly Press, 1988), p. 423. Originally appeared in Gary C. Jacobson, *The Politics of Congressional Elections*, 2nd ed. (Boston: Little, Brown, 1987). Reprinted by permission of Harper Collins Publishers.

election. In the words of Richard Rose, this development is due to several factors:

> First, there is no party system offering reliable support in Congress or public opinion. Second, a President must court the media, for TV newscasters can put the White House on trial any night of the week. A third need, courting Congress, is not a major problem in a parliamentary system, for party discipline normally leads the legislature to endorse what the Cabinet does.[41]

Whereas presidents could once count on political parties to mobilize voters and recruit candidates, unify the legislative efforts of administrators and legislators, and attempt to overcome the stalemate associated with the fragmented policy process[42] by appealing to the importance of party identification, they must now operate in a highly decentralized party system.[43]

A second consequence of the declining role of political parties is that presidents must rely on public support as measured through public opinion polls and must "go public" if Congress is to respond favorably and in a timely fashion to presidential policy initiatives. In an age of increased congressional independence, presidents cannot rely on a disciplined political party in the legislature to deliver votes for administration policy proposals.[44] As a result, it is increasingly difficult for presidents to mobilize our labyrinth-like lawmaking process into action.

The declining role of political parties can be viewed from another perspective, however. John Bibby has argued that strong party unity in Congress will also foster stalemate and gridlock, while a weak party system permits congressional members to cross party lines in order to form bipartisan coalitions. "The looseness of the American party system," says Bibby, "gives governmental officials substantial flexibility and independence in shaping public policy."[45] From the vantage point of the president, however, a weakened party system in the electorate (reflected in a rise in independents and an increase in split-ticket voting and split electoral outcomes) means that members of Congress will be more likely to respond to their constituents on controversial policy questions rather than to presidential leadership and party loyalty. Increasing congressional fragmentation and member independence is the hallmark of a divided government, in which one party controls the executive and the other the legislature. This division promotes the systemic gridlock that has led recent presidential scholars to lament the impossible presidency and to offer major structural reforms designed to build the governing coalitions needed to respond to pressing public policy questions.

The extension of the rhetorical presidency through "going public" and media manipulation has also had dire consequences for the citizenry. Citizens have come to associate strong presidential leadership with a president's ability to speak forcefully and to offer a commanding presence on television. In the age of television, presidential images are far more important than the substance of public policy initiatives. This is true of both presidential campaigns and presidential governance in the electronic plebiscitary age. The political socialization of the citizenry is thus reinforced by the president and his media handlers. This has led one scholar to assert that "today the mass media are a major, if not the leading, cause in making the presidency an impossible challenge."[46]

In the absence of the cohesive political parties necessary for building governing coalitions in a highly fragmented policy process, presidents will be hard pressed to meet heightened citizen expectations of presidential performance in the form of concrete policy accomplishments. Perhaps the greatest contribution of the Reagan presidency to the development of presidential power was Ronald Reagan's ability to maintain high personal popularity despite low presidential success scores with Congress (see Figure 3.1). One explanation for this development is that the public was so mesmerized by Reagan's personality, his appeal to shared American values, and his leadership as personified in carefully scripted television settings that they ignored his inability to prompt the system of shared powers into legislative action throughout much of his last six years in office. There is a message for future occupants of the Oval Office: In order to maintain personal popularity, presidents should use the resources associated with the development of the mature rhetorical presidency. The problem, however, is that not all presidents will have an actor's ability to exude, by their very presence, optimism and faith in the American Dream. As the Reagan experience suggests, if presidents wish to meet the demands of the modern, plebiscitary presidency, they must move beyond the rhetorical powers of the office and devote renewed attention to their legislative and administrative strategies.

Notes

1. John Kenneth White, *The New Politics of Old Values* (Hanover, New Hampshire: University Press of New England, 1988), pp. 60-61.

2. Barger, 1984, p. 417.

3. For an excellent discussion of the paradoxes associated with this dual presidential role, see Thomas E. Cronin, "The Paradoxes of the Presidency," in Robert E. DiClerico, ed., *Analyzing the Presidency* (Guilford, Connecticut: The Dushkin Publishing Group, 1985), pp. 64-76.

4. See Martin Levin, "Ask Not What Our Presidents Are 'Really Like'; Ask What We and Our Political Institutions Are Like: A Call for a Politics of Institutions, Not Men," in Walter Dean Burnham and Martha Wagner Weinberg, eds. *American Politics and Public Policy* (Cambridge, Massachusetts: MIT Press, 1978), p. 112.

5. Quoted in Burt Solomon, "Vulnerable to Events," *National Journal* January 6, 1990, Volume 22, p. 6.

6. See George C. Edwards III, *The Public Presidency: The Pursuit of Popular Support* (New York: St. Martin's Press, 1983); Robert D. Hess and Judith V. Torney, *The Development of Political Attitudes in Children* (Garden City, New York: Anchor Books, 1967); David Easton and Jack Dennis, *Children in the Political System: Origins of Political Legitimacy* (New York: McGraw Hill, 1969).

7. Steven J. Wayne, *The Road to the White House*, 2nd ed. (New York: St. Martin's Press, 1984), p. 211.

8. Robert D. Hess and Judith V. Torney, *The Development of Political Attitudes in Children*, p. 45, as cited in Raymond Tatalovich and Byron W. Daynes, *Presidential Power in the United States* (Monterey, California: Brooks/Cole, 1985), p. 96.

9. An excellent summary of these studies can be found in Tatalovich and Daynes, 1985, pp. 96-97. The original studies referred to here are Dean Jaros, Herbert Hirsch, and Federic J. Fleron, Jr., "The Malevolent Leader: Political Socialization in an American Sub-Culture," *American Political Science Review* June 1968, Volume LXII, p. 569, and the work of Robert Coles in his multi-volume set entitled *Children of Crisis* (Boston: Little, Brown, 1967).

10. Fred I. Greenstein, in James David Barber, ed., "What the President Means to Americans," in *Choosing the President* (Englewood Cliffs, New Jersey: Prentice Hall, 1974), pp. 121-147.

11. See Samuel Kernell, Peter W. Sperbicz, and Aaron Wildavsky, "Public Support for Presidents," in Aaron Wildavsky, ed., *Perspectives on the Presidency* (Boston: Little, Brown, 1975), pp. 148-181, as outlined in Hinckley, 1985, p. 23.

12. See Roberta Sigel, "Images of the American Presidency," *Midwest Journal of Political Science* February 1966, Volume 10, pp. 123-127, as cited in Hinckley, 1985, pp. 23-24.

13. I am indebted to Jeffrey B. Abramson, F. Christopher Arterton and Gary R. Orren for developing the concept of the plebiscitary presidency in this manner. For their discussion of the consequences of the electronic plebiscitary presidency for democratic politics and citizenship, see Abramson, Arterton, and Orren, *The Electronic Commonwealth: The Impact of New Media Technologies on Democratic Politics* (New York: Basic Books, 1988), pp. 20-21.

14. See W. Wayne Shannon, "Mr. Reagan Goes to Washington: Teaching Exceptional America," *Public Opinion*, December-January 1982, Volume 4, pp. 13-17.

15. Robert Dallek, *Ronald Reagan: The Politics of Symbolism* (Cambridge, Massachusetts: Harvard University Press, 1984), p. 7.

16. John H. Aldrich and Thomas Weko, "The Presidency and the Election Process: Campaign Strategy, Voting, and Governance," in Michael Nelson, ed., *The Presidency and the Political System*, 2nd ed. (Washington, D.C.: Congressional Quarterly Press, 1988), pp. 251-252.

17. White, 1988, p. 143.

18. Lou Cannon, *President Reagan: The Role of a Lifetime* (New York: Simon and Schuster, 1991), p. 38.

19. See Nelson, 1988, p. 17.

20. Mary E. Stuckey, *The President as Interpreter-in-Chief* (Chatham, New Jersey: Chatham House, 1991), p. 124.

21. William K. Muir, Jr., "The Primacy of Rhetoric," in Fred I. Greenstein, ed., *Leadership in the Modern Presidency* (Cambridge, Massachusetts: Harvard University Press, 1988), p. 262.

22. See Seligman and Covington, 1989, p. 95, for further discussion of this issue.

23. Samuel Kernell, *Going Public: New Strategies of Presidential Leadership* (Washington, D.C.: Congressional Quarterly Press, 1986), p. viii.

24. See Tulis, 1987, p. 147.

25. For a brief discussion of this dual strategy, see John P. Burke, "Presidential Influence and the Budget Process: A Comparative Analysis," in George C. Edwards III, Steven A. Shull, and Norman C. Thomas, eds., *The Presidency and Public Policy Making* (Pittsburgh: University of Pittsburgh Press, 1985), p. 73.

26. See Thomas Ferguson and Joel Rogers, *Right Turn: The Decline of the Democrats and the Future of American Politics* (New York: Hill and Wang, 1986).

27. Quoted in Samuel Kernell, "Campaigning, Governing, and the Contemporary Presidency," in John E. Chubb and Paul E. Peterson, eds., *The New Direction in American Politics* (Washington, D.C.: Brookings Institution, 1985), p. 118.

28. Mark Hertsgaard, *On Bended Knee: The Press and the Reagan Presidency* (New York: Farrar Straus Giroux, 1988), p. 7.

29. Michael Baruch Grossman and Martha Joynt Kumar, *Portraying the President: The White House and the News Media* (Baltimore: Johns Hopkins University Press, 1981), p. 229.

30. See Hertsgaard, 1988, p. 67.

31. Grossman and Kumar, 1983, p. 324.

32. Barilleaux, 1988, p. 136.

33. David S. Broder, "Bush: Quite a Communicator," *Washington Post* May 30, 1990, p. A21.

34. Burt Solomon, "Bush Cultivates the Press Corps . . . Hoping for a Harvest of Good Will," *National Journal* May 5, 1990, Volume 5, p. 1104.

35. George C. Edwards, III "George Bush and the Public Presidency: The Politics of Inclusion," in Collin Campbell, S.J. and Bert A. Rockman, eds., *The Bush Presidency: First Appraisals* (Chatham, New Jersey: Chatham House, 1991), p. 149.

36. James A. Barnes, "Out on his Own," *National Journal* June 6, 1987, Volume 19, p. 1456.

37. Ronald D. Elving, "The Changing Image of President Bush," *Congressional Quarterly* June 2, 1990, Volume 48, p. 1758.

38. Edwards, 1991, p. 146.

39. For a clear statement of the consequences of this development for the presidency, see Seligman and Covington, 1989.

40. See, for example, Morris P. Fiorina, "The Presidency and Congress," in Michael Nelson, ed., *The Presidency and the Political System*, 2nd ed. (Washington, D.C.: Congressional Quarterly Press, 1988), pp. 411-434.

41. Rose, 1989, p. 9.

42. Burns, 1984, p. 135.

43. See George C. Edwards III, *The Public Presidency: The Pursuit of Popular Support* (New York: St. Martin's Press, 1983), p. 203.

44. See Glenn R. Parker, *Characteristics of Congress: Patterns in Congressional Behavior* (Englewood Cliffs, New Jersey: Prentice Hall, 1989), Chapter 9, "Lack of Party Discipline," for further development of this theme. Randall B. Ripley also addresses this theme, but does not emphasize congressional party independence nearly as much as Parker. Ripley concluded that "Despite much commentary to the effect that American political parties are weak both in the electorate and in the national legislature, they are, inside Congress, one of the major potential integrating forces. They do not always realize that potential, but sometimes it can be stimulated by leadership from within the House and Senate or from the White House." See Randall B. Ripley, *Congress: Process and Policy*, 4th ed. (New York: Norton, 1988), pp. 187-189.

45. John F. Bibby, *Politics, Parties, and Elections in America* (Chicago: Nelson Hall, 1987), pp. 352-353.

46. Barger, 1984, p. viii.

4

The Rebirth of the
Administrative Presidency

Article II of the Constitution mandates that the president is responsible for ensuring that the laws passed by Congress are faithfully executed. Recent presidents, however, have found it difficult to exercise policy control over the federal bureaucracy because of its size, its rigidity, and its firmly established ties to congressional interests. Perhaps former President Jimmy Carter put it best: "Before I became president, I realized and was warned that dealing with the federal bureaucracy would be one of the worst problems I would have to face. It has been worse than I had anticipated."[1] Carter's concern has also been explored in King and Ragsdale's recent work, which examines the illusion of presidential governance. They conclude that "although the illusion that they function as solitary individuals drives presidents first to seek policy control and then to enlarge administrative organizations in an effort to gain it, presidents are often unable to surmount the constraints of coequal branches of Congress and the bureaucracy."[2] The logic and structure of their positions in a highly fragmented administrative branch forces presidents to delegate authority.[3]

The purpose of this chapter is to assess how the Reagan administration dealt with these structural constraints of the presidency and to identify a possible bureaucratic strategy for future presidents in light of the Reagan experience. The Reagan administration pursued an administrative strategy characterized by centralization and politicization in the absence of the coherent political parties needed for coalition-building efforts.[4] This chapter examines Reagan's use of the presidential appointment process as one element of his administrative presidency; it also details how he attempted to pursue additional presidential administrative strategies, including his skillful use of the budgetary reconciliation process, executive orders, and central clearance. The early Bush administrative strategy can be analyzed by comparing it to Reagan's approach to the executive branch. The intent is to raise questions about sources of presidential power in light of the Reagan and early Bush experiences with the bureaucracy. This chapter will also synthesize and attempt to bring order to the recent presidency literature that examines the administrative presidency in the Reagan and Bush eras.

The Historical Context for the Administrative Presidency

Franklin Delano Roosevelt entered office in 1932 and faced the economic and social problems of the 1930s with an administrative structure that was better equipped to deal with the problems of the nineteenth century. Roosevelt had promised reorganization of the executive branch during his 1932 presidential campaign and reinforced this promise in his first presidential press conference.[5] Yet his promise was not carried out until his second presidential term.

The Brownlow Commission, appointed by Roosevelt on March 22, 1936, was created for the purpose of examining the problem of administrative management.[6] In 1937, President Roosevelt's Committee on Administrative Management concluded that "the President needs help." In response, Congress passed a law authorizing the 1939 Roosevelt reorganization plan creating the Executive Office of the President, which resulted in considerable enlargement in presidential staff through the years. The Brownlow Commission's final report included the following recommendations:

1. To deal with the greatly increased duties of executive management falling upon the president the White House staff should be expanded.
2. The managerial agencies of the Government, particularly those dealing with the budget, efficiency research, personnel, and planning, should be greatly strengthened and developed as arms of the Chief Executive.
3. The merit system should be extended upward, outward, and downward to cover all non-policy-determining posts, and the civil service system should be reorganized and opportunities established for a career system attractive to the best talent of the Nation.
4. The whole Executive Branch of the Government should be overhauled and the present 100 agencies reorganized under a few

large departments in which every executive activity would find its place.

5. The fiscal system should be extensively revised in the light of the best governmental and private practice, particularly with reference to financial records, audit, and accountability of the Executive to the Congress.[7]

Congress rejected most of the Brownlow recommendations. Many congressional members felt that if the Brownlow reform suggestions were enacted, far too much power would accrue to the executive branch. Yet as John Hart points out, "What Brownlow did was provide the catalyst for the first serious congressional response to the critical problem of presidential work load."[8] Congress ultimately incorporated only two of the committee's proposals as a part of the Reorganization Act of 1939: "(a) continuous reorganization authority for the President, qualified in the legislation . . . by provision for a congressional veto and by exemptions of some agencies; and (b) provision of six 'administrative assistants' to the President."[9] By passing the Reorganization Act of 1939, Congress provided the president with the authority to submit executive branch reorganization plans,[10] which ultimately led to the creation of the Executive Office of the President (see Figure 4.1).

In passing the Reorganization Act of 1939, Congress provided considerable institutional support to the presidency, and as we will see soon, future presidents reaped the benefits. The administrative reforms of the late 1930s meant that all presidents since Franklin Roosevelt have had the freedom to create a variety of approaches to manage the bureaucracy and meet staffing needs. It is important to recognize, however, that the Brownlow Commission reform suggestions did not anticipate that any occupant of the Oval Office would exercise such monumental administrative prerogative powers.

With the creation of the Executive Office of the President in 1939, the president was awarded five separate units: the Bureau of the Budget, the White House, and three World War II agencies (the National Resources Planning Board, the Liaison Office for Personnel Management, and the Office of Government Reports). Over the years, some forty different councils, boards, and offices have made up this office. Since 1939, then, presidents have had an administrative structure, created by Congress, that has been directly responsive to presidential interests.[11] Yet as the Executive Office of the President has increased in size and scope, it has also challenged presidents to devise administrative strategies for oversight and control. The Reagan approach to administrative management offers some practical suggestions for future presidents as they attempt to control the organizationally autonomous executive branch.

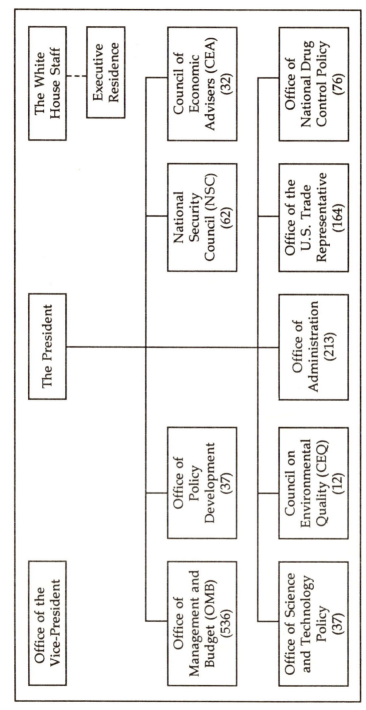

FIGURE 4.1 Executive Office of the President.   *Source: The United States Government Manual 1987–1988* (Washington, DC: Government Printing Office, 1987), p. 86.

The implementation of some of the Brownlow recommendations has meant tremendous changes in the administrative apparatus of presidential governance. One consequence is that the White House staff has become "a permanent, reasonably specialized, and highly expandable institution."[12]   A second consequence is that with the increase in presidential administrative resources, greater demands are placed on the presidency itself. Presidents have been forced to turn to the appointment process in an effort to meet these heightened expectations of presidential performance. Third, given the tremendous growth in the federal bureaucracy since the late 1930s and the resulting problems that presidents face in controlling the policy implementation process in a highly fragmented political system, presidents have embraced a managerial strategy for governance.[13]

In addition to the creation of the Executive Office of the President and the increase in presidential staff, presidents have been awarded help in several other ways. The creation of the Office of Management and Budget, an extension of the Bureau of the Budget, was meant to strengthen presidential involvement in the budgetary process. New sources of presidential power were provided by Congress in defense and military power arenas with the creation of the Joint Chiefs of Staff, the CIA, and the FBI. Congress has also given help to presidents in the form of "emergency powers." And since the 1930s, Congress has continuously given discretion to presidents in legislation that grants vague authority to the executive branch for policy implementation.[14] Presidents have learned that in the absence of cohesive party organizations, these important powers, sanctioned by Congress, have allowed the Executive Office of the President and the White House to play integral political and policymaking roles. These powers are especially important given the increasing fragmentation of Congress. Yet for Ronald Reagan, it was a dual approach to presidential governance that characterized his administrative strategy and set the tone for his White House organization and interaction with senior cabinet officials. Unlike Nixon, who began his presidency by pursuing a legislative approach at first and then switching to a centralized administrative strategy, the Reagan administration pursued a dual strategy from the beginning.[15] According to Richard Nathan, administrative action is characterized by a president "using the discretion permitted in the implementation of existing laws rather than advancing these policy aims through the enactment of new legislation."[16]   Reagan used both legislative and administrative actions to pursue his policy goals of cutting government spending and eliminating federal government intrusion in the social policy arena.[17] In so doing, he exercised presidential power sources in ways that suggest possible new directions for future presidents as they attempt to translate their campaign promises into concrete public policy.

Reagan's Use of the Appointment Power

The presidential appointment power is an important resource that presidents can use to pursue their policy goals. Given that Congress has continually provided executive officials with broad latitude and discretion in enforcing and implementing laws, presidential appointments have taken on new importance. If presidents hope to influence the policy implementation process, they must rely on the people that they have appointed to various executive agencies. Each new administration can make as many as 3,000 appointments, and many of these appointments can affect presidential policy success.[18]   There are a number of reasons, however, that presidents find it increasingly difficult to control the executive branch through personnel management and the presidential appointment process. Those responsible for administering the presidential personnel process, including the president, are often in office for only four years, and this has proved to be too short a period for understanding personnel management. Second, presidents soon find that Congress also plays an integral role in determining the shape and structure of the federal personnel system. Congress is responsible for establishing benefit and pay levels, as well as for setting personnel ceilings for individual agencies. In addition, the Senate must approve presidential appointments. Third, there are few successful models of personnel management from previous administrations for a new president to copy.   Fourth, presidents find it difficult to build the necessary governing coalitions through presidential appointments because of the "peculiar interweaving of politics and administration that is characteristic of our political system"[19] and the fact that once they take office, political appointees face numerous crosspressures from the president, Congress, and interest groups.[20]   Fifth, newly elected presidents learn that their appointing authority must be used to meet the demands of groups who supported their candidacies throughout the primary and general election seasons. As Francis Rourke has suggested, these individuals feel "that they are entitled to high-level representation in an administration they have helped to put in office."[21]   Sixth, presidents are also confronted with the need to placate those constituencies that were not part of their electoral and campaign support. Presidents can use the political appointment process, then, to appease those groups who were not originally members of the electoral coalition. Seventh, there is no guarantee that those individuals who the president appoints will adhere to the administration's goals and actively support key policy initiatives.

Presidents might be better equipped to use the appointment process to their advantage if they implemented their strategy in a timely and efficient manner during the transition period.[22] The literature on presidential transitions suggests that a president must "hit the ground running" with respect to the personnel operation and appointment process. This means that presidential candidates should be thinking about their potential appointments even before the election. A presidential candidate must, however, be careful to avoid two potential pitfalls in this area. First, the names of potential appointees must not leak out, for fear of alienating those supporters who might not be selected. Second, attention might be drawn away from the campaign if the media catch wind of possible presidential appointments. There is a danger, too, that the media might portray a candidate as overconfident if steps are taken during the campaign to prepare for presidential governance.[23] This analysis says nothing, however, about the importance of allowing the voting electorate to consider a president's likely administrative strategy as a way to make a more informed presidential choice. Surely a case can be made for having presidential candidates announce their cabinet and chief advisors during the campaign as a way to give citizens more of an opportunity to evaluate the candidates' judgment and potential White House managerial styles. In this way, more attention could be devoted to the substance of candidate approaches to governance rather than to the symbolism and vague pronouncements that have characterized recent presidential campaigns during the television age.

Like the Kennedy, Johnson, and Nixon administrations, the Reagan transition team used task forces during the transition period. What distinguished the Reagan approach, however, was that he staffed them with ideological partisans. As Terry Moe reports, "Their task was to gain inside information on the operation and organization of specific agencies, to which they had virtually unfettered access granted by the Carter administration."[24] Their reports and recommendations were instrumental as the Reagan team implemented plans for the new presidency.

Under the direction of E. Pendleton James, the Reagan administration centralized personnel appointments throughout the executive branch and filled positions largely on partisan grounds; appointments were based on ideological and programmatic positions on key political issues.[25] Students of the Reagan personnel selection process have generally agreed that James and his subordinates adhered to five selection criteria: compatibility with the president's conservative approach to government; integrity (although this criteria must be questioned in light of the dubious backgrounds of many of the Reagan appointees as well as their performances once in office); toughness; competence; and a commitment to being a team player.[26] As Bradley Patterson points out, "All non-career/political personnel were expected to have voted in the 1980 election and to have given some level of support to the Reagan/Bush campaign or to a candidate for another office who supported Reagan/Bush."[27] Many of those who were appointed to agency leadership positions lacked relevant experience and were also openly hostile to their agencies and the notion of federal government involvement.   In the interview process, lower-level appointees had been socialized thoroughly by Reagan aides and the conservative task forces about the need to implement a conservative ideological perspective upon entering office.[28]   The Office of Presidential Personnel (OPP) played a greater role in the early stages of the Reagan administration than it had in any other previous administration.[29] Presidential scholar G. Calvin Mackenzie has written that James "provided an unprecedented thread of consistency throughout the entire staffing of the Reagan administration" as, "the most stalwart protector . . . of a policy of centralized control of presidential appointments."[30]

The Reagan appointment process achieved its goal of producing a largely monolithic set of appointees to the executive branch. Virtually all of the key Reagan appointees shared the president's conservative approach to government and were largely committed to goals that he articulated in his presidential campaign. They were also alike to the extent that they represented the wealthiest class in American society. Critics questioned whether individuals who were so removed from the mainstream of American life could possibly represent the majority of Americans' views. Of course, this became more important as Reagan pursued a policy of domestic fiscal retrenchment and a massive defense buildup at the expense of the working class.[31]

Reagan's appointment strategy was used as a vehicle for promoting the administration's policies through the legislative process and the media. Individuals appointed to various government agencies controlled spending, regulatory, and personnel decisions almost from the outset.[32] They controlled spending decisions by placing many special domestic projects that were left over from the Carter administration on hold, "and shifting contracts and grants to recipients felt to be in agreement with Reagan's conservative policies."[33] This approach represented a major point of departure from previous administrations and was an important component of the Reagan.attempt to translate campaign promises into concrete public policy.

Reagan's Use of the Budgetary Process

Much of Ronald Reagan's success in the domestic policy arena can be attributed to the clarity and consistency of his message to "cut domestic spending, increase defense spending, and limit federal regulation."[34] In a 1976 speech to the Executive Club of Chicago, then candidate Reagan articulated clearly his hostility toward excessive federal government involvement, a hostility that became an underlying tenet of his presidential campaigns and presidency: "Virtually all economic and social ailments stem from a single source—the belief that government, particularly the federal government, has the answer to our ills."[35] The answer, from Reagan's perspective, was to rely on state and local governments and the private sector to fill the breach when federal government intrusion was eliminated.

The federal budget process was the central vehicle used by the Reagan administration to translate its philosophical beliefs into public policy. The reconciliation process had first been used successfully in 1980 by the Carter administration, but the Reagan team forced Congress to adhere to most of the President's spending requests by emphasizing "a highly centralized, top-down approach to federal budgeting, which left little room for agency input."[36] David Stockman employed budget reconciliation to excellent effect in 1981. Stockman's budget plan required almost all appropriations and authorizing committees to act on policy changes and spending cuts. The cuts approved for Fiscal Year 1982, most of which were in entitlement programs, were adopted in a single "up-or-down" vote in both the House and the Senate.[37] This meant that members of Congress would be on record either supporting or opposing a popular, newly elected president. Congressional budget expert Allen Schick characterizes budgetary reconciliation in the following way:

> It offers an integrated and expedited consideration of proposed reductions. Rather than splitting the president's recommendations into numerous separate measures, reconciliation provides for most of them to be combined into a single bill. And rather than allowing legislative activity to proceed at its usual unhurried pace, reconciliation establishes deadlines for the development of legislation by various congressional committees. Most important, the central purpose of reconciliation is to conform existing laws to current budget policies, thus providing Congress with an instrument for implementing the president's budget reductions.[38]

Stockman's superb use of the reconciliation strategy in Reagan's first year transformed the power of the president vis-à-vis Congress in the budgetary process.[39] The 1974 Budget Act had been transformed because the president now had the power to discipline Congress and force serious consideration of budgetary priorities.[40] This approach allowed the administration to articulate a coherent policy vision as well as to catch interest groups, bureaucrats, and members of Congress by surprise. As the Reagan experience indicates, presidents can use the budget as a central tool for governing by endorsing or rejecting specific policies. Control of the budgetary process, then, is an important presidential prerogative power available to all presidents.

The euphoria of Reagan's first year budgetary accomplishments did not last for long, however, as the most serious recession since the Great Depression enveloped the nation in the middle of 1981. Unemployment rose to its highest level since the early 1930s, interest rates skyrocketed, and the federal budget deficit doubled within two years. The administration began to lose control of the budgetary process to a much more aggressive Congress. After 1981, Reagan and his advisors had much less success in cutting domestic spending and limiting the growth of entitlement through the reconciliation process. This was undoubtedly due to the prevailing belief that increased cutbacks would threaten "the social safety net," and make it difficult for congressional members to achieve re-election in the face of high unemployment and recession conditions. It was in this context that members of Congress, some of President Reagan's own administration officials, and leading economists began to attack the growing federal deficit. Congress attempted to force the White House into deficit-cutting action by passing the Gramm-Rudman-Hollings legislation in 1985.

The Reagan budgetary experience suggests that future presidents may well be able to exercise greater control of the American policy process by implementing the budgetary reconciliation strategy. This is especially true in a time of fiscal retrenchment. Commenting on the Reagan budgetary approach, Richard Waterman writes: "Record high budget deficits increased the Reagan administration's ability to demand cuts in the programs that it opposed. This was particularly important when it came to justifying cuts in popular programs, as the administration was able to argue that deep budget cuts were necessary for the good of the economy as a whole."[41]

The Reagan administrative strategy also suggests, however, that presidents who rely on budgetary procedures as a way to influence administrative behavior will likely confront numerous barriers. Presidents are greatly limited in their choice of programs to cut. Much of the federal budget is composed of entitlement programs (including Medicare and Social Security) that have strict legislative benefit-level requirements. If these programs are to be modified, they will require new legislative initiatives.[42] In addition, as Ronald Reagan learned, interest groups are powerful stabilizing forces in the American policy process and work diligently to protect their chosen programs. Despite recent research suggesting that subgovernments may be on the wane in certain policy areas, "cozy triangles" play important roles in insuring that bureaucratic agencies, interest groups, and members of Congress reap the benefits of federal spending.

Reagan's Use of Executive Orders and Central Clearance

Another source of presidential prerogative power is the use of executive orders. In the face of a fragmented and more independent Congress, presidents have used executive orders as important sources of presidential power. Reagan imposed Executive Order 12291 as a major regulatory review requirement in an effort to gain greater control over administrative rulemaking. This executive order insured that Reagan would have greater control over executive agencies because they were now "required to prepare analyses of proposed regulations and to submit these analyses to the Office of Management and Budget for review."[43] In addition, the order stipulated that all program review and justification must proceed in terms of cost-benefit analysis. Executive Order 12291 was a particularly impressive way for a president to gain control over spending by an increasingly fragmented bureaucracy. William F. West and Joseph Cooper have even argued that "in response to the limitations of earlier orders, it has established the most rigorous analytical requirements and the most comprehensive and powerful executive review mechanism to date."[44]

Administrative rulemaking and clearance were used successfully by the Reagan administration to pursue its policy goals. As Executive Order 12291 makes clear, central clearance is one of the most formidable instruments of presidential control over the bureaucracy. President Coolidge began the practice in 1921 when he issued a directive that required "all departments and agencies to clear their budget proposals with the Bureau of the Budget to ensure their compatibility with the president's own budget priorities."[45] Franklin Roosevelt extended the practice even further when he demanded that all legislation emanating from the bureaucracy be subject to screening procedures. Reagan instituted a mandatory review of all major rules and spending decisions that was particularly useful in monitoring regulatory activity. As it has developed over time, central clearance is an institutionalized review process that insures that all departmental, agency, and commission legislative proposals are reviewed before they are sent to Congress. This use of presidential prerogative power was grounded firmly in two phases of Article II of the Constitution: "take care that the Laws be faithfully executed" and "Executive Power shall be vested in a

President."[46]   This is an area that warrants further attention by presidency scholars as they attempt to bring greater coherence to the literature.

Reagan's Approach to Cabinet Governance

Reflecting upon the failures of the Carter presidency, Reagan, the presidential candidate, said, "The problem with Carter is that he tries to do everything at once and he tries to do too much of it himself. If we win we are going to set priorities and do things one at a time."[47] Given his aversion to Carter's centralized style of decisionmaking, Reagan, like many of his predecessors, expressed firm support for cabinet governance. As he introduced his cabinet appointees on December 20, 1980, Reagan said: "I am more confident than ever that cabinet government can and will work."[48] Unlike Presidents Nixon and Carter, Reagan reduced the role of the White House staff in policy development and turned to the Cabinet for advice in policy decisions.[49]

Yet like many presidents before him, Reagan soon departed from the goal of a cabinet government. As numerous presidential scholars have pointed out, Reagan headed "one of the most White House centralized administrations in history."[50] Reagan began his presidency with a White House organization that was dominated by three people who had direct and continuous access to the president—James Baker, Michael Deaver, and Edwin Meese. This arrangement was referred to as "the troika," "the triumvirate," and "the three-headed monster." Baker, as chief of staff, tended to have the greatest policy access to the president.[51]   During Reagan's first year, there was considerable jockeying among the three for the president's attention, and jealous turf battles erupted. By Reagan's second term, Deaver and Meese had left the White House and Donald Regan had replaced James Baker as chief of staff. With Regan's appointment came a tightly controlled, centralized, and hierarchical organizational style. Presidential centralization was reinforced by Reagan's control of budgetary priorities through central clearance and by his tight control over political appointments.

At the same time, however, the Reagan administration offered an important contribution to cabinet governance by creating a cabinet council system. Reagan reacted to the chaotic organization of the Carter White House by establishing "a focused, ideological policy apparatus."[52] Unlike Jimmy Carter and George Bush, Reagan had a clearly developed ideological view of the world that undoubtedly contributed to his White House organization. This view is reflected in the cabinet council approach developed by Edwin Meese.

The Reagan administration created seven cabinet councils in the first term, all of which were constructed around specific issues: Economic Affairs, Human Resources, Natural Resources and Environment, Food and Agriculture, Commerce and Trade, Legal Policy, and Management and Administration. Domestic advisor Martin Anderson offered this overview of Reagan's cabinet council system:

> A cabinet council was really a smaller, tailor-made version of the cabinet. Each cabinet council was designed to deal with certain specific issues of national policy. When a cabinet council met it had the same force and authority in dealing with those issues as the entire cabinet did. The members of the cabinet councils were selected primarily on the basis that the departments they headed were deeply involved in the specific issues that would be discussed at the cabinet council meetings.[53]

Anderson contends that the cabinet council system worked well because it "could deal effectively with national issues that cut across two or more departments."[54] As chairman of each cabinet council, Reagan merely established the ideological vision and then assumed that his carefully chosen appointees would adhere to the clearly articulated principles of his presidential campaign. By his second term, however, the Reagan cabinet council system was in disarray. The seven-council system of his first term was too unwieldy, and as a result, it was reduced to a three-council system in the second term: Domestic, Economic, and National Security. This new structure was more workable (at least at the outset of the second term) because it provided forums for cabinet secretaries to work with colleagues who had overlapping responsibilities and with White House staff members who had responsibilities in the same policy areas. By the end of Reagan's second term, however, many of the cabinet councils fell into disuse and one study concluded that they had little actual impact on the outcome of policy even in Reagan's first term. Instead, they tended to facilitate the implementation of policies on the agenda rather than engaging in policy formulation and development.[55] Of course, active participation in policy implementation by Reagan officials committed to the administration's conservative ideological outlook proved to be an important attempt to insure that campaign promises were translated into concrete policy results.

Underlying all of these efforts was Reagan's commitment to a detached style of governance as well as a willingness to prioritize his administration policy goals.[56] Reagan's prioritizing was described by former White House executive official Ben W. Heineman: "A key element of the strategy of governing is the division of domestic issues into first, second and third order initiatives. If the Reagan Presidency has shown anything, it has demonstrated the importance of having the

President focus on a few key issues."[57] Undoubtedly, the clarity of his ideological message, the support of his White House administrative apparatus, and his willingness to prioritize contributed to Reagan's policy success early in his first term. He also received praise for his chairman-of-the-board style of daily management until the Iran-Contra affair story broke in November 1987. Reagan's willingness to delegate authority was reflected in his response to a reporter's question regarding how he decides which problems to address personally and which to leave to subordinates:

> You surround yourself with the best people you can find, delegate authority, and don't interfere as long as the overall policy that you've decided upon is being carried out. In the Cabinet meetings—and some members of the Cabinet who have been members of other Cabinets told me there had never been such meetings—I use a system in which I want to hear what everybody wants to say honestly. I want the decisions made on what is right or wrong, what is good or bad for the people of this country. I encourage all the input I can get. . . . And when I've heard all that I need to make a decision, I don't take a vote. I make the decision. Then I expect every one of them, whether their views have carried the day or not, to go forward together in carrying out the policy.[58]

Reagan's managerial style is best characterized as one of risk and inattention to detail. This quickly became apparent during his infrequent press conferences, which were characterized by numerous "gaffes" and an inability to answer questions about his policies in a coherent way. His press secretaries, Larry Speakes and Marlin Fitzwater, were often forced to engage in "spin control" in an effort to contain the damage of Reagan's press conference misstatements.[59] Throughout his presidency, Reagan consistently demonstrated a profound lack of knowledge about policy concerns that were central to his legislative agenda. But it wasn't until the Iran-Contra affair that students of the presidency began to describe a presidency out of control; and Reagan's laissez-faire style of management received much of the blame. Stephen Hess has persuasively argued that when Reagan's views were not clearly articulated, members of his administration were forced to rely on guesswork, and a system that had worked well at the outset of his administration began to lose its overall effectiveness.[60]

The Bush Approach to the Executive Branch

The early Bush administrative strategy represents a significant departure from that of his predecessor. Ronald Reagan was a president with a clearly defined ideology that was consistently applied to specific policy issues. Reagan's clarity of purpose enabled him to identify those individuals who might best serve him in positions of power throughout the executive branch. George Bush, however, failed to develop a clear ideology in his presidential campaign, and this has been reflected in his own ambiguous views on key issues including abortion, the deficit, the environment, and education. This lack of ideological vision has had several consequences for the Bush presidency.

First, President Bush has been reduced to offering a variety of platitudes, including being the "education" and "environmental" president, and the importance of developing "a kinder, gentler nation." These pronouncements have largely replaced substantive policy initiatives. Of course, this should come as no surprise, given that Bush's candidacy centered largely on the symbolism of the American flag and the racist symbolism of Willie Horton rather than articulating on meaningful and substantive policy issues. Second, when he enjoyed very high public opinion ratings in a longer-than-usual presidential honeymoon, Bush squandered valuable opportunities to offer bold and creative policy leadership on the issues of the day. Unlike Reagan, Bush had a small legislative agenda and his advisors eschewed the "One Hundred Days" strategy.[61] This was done to reduce the already heightened expectations that accompany any president's honeymoon period. Another explanation for Bush's congressional strategy is the party composition of Congress. Recent empirical work on Congress has stressed the importance of political party control to a president's ability to translate campaign promises into concrete public policy.[62] This important leadership resource was missing during Bush's first term: The Democrats had a ten-seat advantage in the Senate and an eighty-five-seat advantage in the House. These majorities were slightly larger than those that characterized the Reagan era.

Several other factors proved important in evaluating the early Bush presidency. The 1980 and 1984 presidential elections gave Ronald Reagan the perception of a mandate. George Bush's 1988 electoral victory hardly compared to Reagan's convincing wins over Jimmy Carter and Walter Mondale. Bush's 53 percent victory margin was unimpressive, the Republican party lost seats in both the House and Senate, and he trailed almost all representatives and senators in their constituencies.[63]

Bush did enjoy several advantages in succeeding a president of his own party and one that he served as vice-president. These advantages manifested themselves throughout the transition period and during his first two years in office. He obviously had Reagan's help and support and benefitted from the Republican party loyalists who held leadership positions throughout the executive branch. Several members of Reagan's executive branch played central roles in the Bush campaign and in his cabinet. At the same time, Bush faced problems in succeeding a popular president of his own party. Bush had to establish his own administration and style of governing; he had to allow for his own appointments without dismissing Republican party and Reagan loyalists too quickly; and most importantly, he had to establish his own policy direction without appearing to repudiate the policies of Ronald Reagan.[64]

Bush has also been hamstrung by the whopping federal deficit left to him by his predecessor. The deficit and the Gramm-Rudman-Hollings legislation have constrained the Bush administration in several ways. Bush and his budget director Richard Darman considered the Fiscal Year 1990 and 1991 budgets within the politics of retrenchment and fiscal austerity as they attempted to meet the Gramm-Rudman-Hollings yearly deficit ceilings. Little room was left for new policy initiatives, especially given the administration's promise of "no new taxes" and the fact that money had to be spent to deal with several instances of mismanagement and scandal left by the Reagan administration. These spending initiatives included rescuing the savings and loan system, dealing with the fiscal disaster at the Department of Housing and Urban Development, and cleaning up nuclear production plants. Like Reagan, Bush was forced to present the appearance of deficit reduction through the use of accounting gimmicks.[65]

Bush has also had more than his share of difficulties in staffing his new administration. One might have expected that he would have very few staffing problems, given his Washington experience and his friends both inside and outside of government. Yet it took Bush longer than any other postwar president to name his cabinet, and he was very slow in naming the remainder of his administration. Early in Bush's tenure, there was a perception that he was wasting valuable time in his honeymoon period—a waste that would undermine his policy proposals. This was hardly an issue, however, because the newly elected Bush administration did not have much of a policy agenda to pursue.

Presidential scholar G. Calvin Mackenzie has identified several factors that contributed to Bush's inability to staff his administration in a timely manner. First, the nature of the appointment process itself is fraught with procedural delays, including ethics reviews, FBI background checks, political references, and congressional clearances. Second, the Bush transition team failed to engage in the necessary clear and aggressive planning that characterized the Reagan transition effort. Third, Bush was hampered by a much larger-than-usual number of potential appointees rejecting the offer to join his administration. This can be attributed to the fact that the congressional vote against the pay raise in the early days of the new Congress deterred some individuals from joining the executive bureaucracy.[66] From this vantage point, then, perhaps all newly elected presidents will face the same sort of problems that plagued the Bush transition team in appointing qualified individuals to the executive branch.

Bush's own efforts were hampered by his continued support of the nomination of his long-time friend John Tower to head the Department of Defense in the face of mounting congressional and media opposition. His misguided support of Tower had two major consequences. First, the delay caused by the Tower nomination battle kept some forty appointed positions vacant at the Pentagon.[67] This provided ammunition to those critics who argued that Bush's tenure in office was off to a rocky beginning. Second, the Tower affair undermined Bush's relationship with Congress. Despite his modest legislative agenda, Bush had done well in establishing a positive and cordial relationship with Congress. As a former member of the House and having recently presided over the Senate, Bush had many friends on both sides of the aisle. Almost all senators and more than half of the members of the House had been invited to the White House for some function during the first half of 1989.[68] In sharp contrast to Jimmy Carter and even to Ronald Reagan, Bush devoted considerable energy to establishing positive communication channels with Congress. The Tower affair undermined this atmosphere of good feeling because Bush allowed the unsuccessful nomination battle to dominate the early months of his new administration. Bush did receive some positive press for showing "toughness," thus bolstering his image in the important presidential-expectation game, and for displaying loyalty to a long-time friend. One advisor confirmed this assessment of Bush's character: "George Bush is very loyal to people, more than to ideas."[69] But in the end, valuable time that could have been devoted to working with Congress on key policies, including AIDS, energy and the environment, education, and the deficit was lost to the administration's full scale press on behalf of John Tower's nomination. Fortunately for Bush, the Senate quickly confirmed his second choice for secretary of defense, former Ford Chief of Staff Richard Cheney.

Bush, adopting the cabinet council system of Reagan's second term, established three cabinet councils: Economic Policy, chaired by Treasury Secretary Brady; Domestic Policy, chaired by Attorney General Richard Thornburgh and National Security, chaired by the president's advisor for national security, Brent Scowcroft. Assistant to the President for Economic and Domestic Policy Roger Porter designed Bush's policy development process by establishing a "multiple advocacy" model.[70]

This highly structured decisionmaking process allows the president to hear his top advisors argue about the various policy alternatives regarding a particular issue. Porter contends that this model worked successfully during the Ford administration and that his new boss's personality is amenable to such success again. While multiple advocacy is time consuming and difficult to manage, it does allow the president to hear members of his cabinet debate the issues of the day. As Bush pointed out midway through his first term: "I've known pretty well how I want to reach decisions—get good, strong, experienced people, encourage them to express their views openly, encourage them not to hold back. . . . I've been to Cabinet meetings when [they have] been a show-and-tell. We don't do ours that way."[71] It is interesting to note that George Bush did not offer the usual ringing endorsement of cabinet government during his campaign; yet ironically, when compared to other presidents since Dwight Eisenhower, Bush may well be coming closest to putting such a vision into practice.

Bush's appointments to the cabinet and White House staff reflect his Washington and Republican party insider status and reveal a commitment to rewarding friends and close confidants. Bush's team is largely moderate to conservative in ideology, experienced in Washington policymaking, monolithic, and strongly tied to the establishment. Some have pointed out that the Bush administration better reflects Gerald Ford's approach to governance than Ronald Reagan's. Presidential scholar Fred Greenstein said: "It's manifestly a mainstream politician back in Washington. Not since Jerry Ford have we seen that."[72] It is also clear that this administration's policymakers have ties to one another. One Bush aide concluded that the Bush Cabinet and White House staff is characterized by "an Administration of colleagues, not . . . of strangers."[73] Bush's team resembles Reagan's to the extent that both administration's appointments were men and women of wealth and property. One report concluded that financial disclosure documents filed by Bush's appointees revealed "that many Cabinet members and other high-ranking officials—and, in some cases, their spouses—retain significant holdings in the corporate sector."[74] Their homogeneous backgrounds have prompted others to question whether they fairly represent the concerns of the lower and middle classes. This is important because Bush comes from a background that brings into question his ability to understand the plight of those outside the elite upper class.

While Bush has largely shunned policy ideologues such as James G. Watt or Anne Gorsuch Burford, he has received mixed reviews in his environmental appointments. William K. Reilly, Bush's appointment to head the Environmental Protection Agency, received wide praise by environmentalists. Some questioned the influence Reilly would have on environmental matters in a Bush administration. This concern was heightened early in his first term when reports leaked to the press that it was John Sununu, and not Reilly, who had Bush's ear on key environmental matters. Others argued that at best, the Bush appointments in environmental policy reflected a mixed record on environmental matters. For example, there was outspoken criticism of James E. Cason's appointment as Assistant Secretary of Agriculture for Natural Resources and the Environment.[75] On the whole, however, Bush appeared to de-emphasize ideological loyalty in his appointments when compared to the Reagan appointment approach. For George Bush, personal loyalty was much more important than ideological loyalty. At the same time, none of the Bush appointments had achieved solid liberal or progressive records on key domestic or foreign policy issues.

No discussion of the early Bush approach to governing would be complete without a brief overview of the role of his first chief of staff, John Sununu. From the beginning, Sununu served as an important ideological liaison to the conservative wing of the Republican party. Sununu joined Vice-President Quayle in attempting to appease those right-wing elements of the Republican party that have never trusted Bush's politics. Sununu solicited their views on the key issues of the day and attempted to appoint their candidates to central second-level administrative posts. For example, he succeeded in placing staunch opponents of abortion at the Department of Health and Human Services.[76] He also played an important lightning-rod role in the Bush administration: Sununu was more than willing to take the heat for unpopular Bush policies, including recent anti-environmental decisions and the nomination of David Souter to replace Justice Brennan on the United States Supreme Court. But when Sununu blamed the president for a so-called ad-libbed "remark about credit card interest rates that started a chain of events and sent the stock market skidding" in mid-November 1991, Sununu paved the way for his own removal, for he had contributed to the impression that President Bush himself was confused about how to deal with the troubled economy.[77] Sununu was replaced by Secretary Samuel Skinner, who was regarded as less combative and more likely to work as a conciliatory team player.

Yet it would be a mistake to assume that Sununu was a "strong" chief of staff in the mold of former Eisenhower Chief of Staff Sherman Adams or Reagan second term Chief of Staff Donald Regan. James Pfiffner points out that after six months in office, "Sununu spent about one third of his time with the President and did not seem to act as a strict gatekeeper for access to the President." Much of this was due to George Bush's presidential style, which stressed personal contact with people in and outside of the administration. He tended to deal with his cabinet secretaries directly, rather than through his chief of staff as had President Reagan.[78] Recent events, however, indicate that Pfiffner may have underestimated Sununu's role and influence in the Bush administration. Evidence suggests, for example, that Sununu played a central role in persuading George Bush to nominate David Souter to the Supreme Court[79] and to adopt a more conservative line on acid rain policy. Regardless of the actual role played by Sununu in the Bush administration, Bush has largely avoided the petty in-fighting that characterized the Carter and Reagan White House staffs. In this sense, he has received high marks for choosing a cabinet and White House staff loyal to the President.

In sum, George Bush hit the ground coasting, rather than running, in his efforts to establish an administrative strategy. This was befitting a president-elect who followed a popular president of his own party, one whom he had served dutifully as vice-president for eight years. It should come as no surprise, then, that Bush approached Congress and the bureaucracy from the vantage point of consolidation and reactive problem solving, rather than from the standpoint of an ideological vision. Whether such a minimalist approach is viable, given the budget deficit, AIDS, education, housing, the environment, and a whole host of foreign policy concerns, is a question ripe for critical discussion. But perhaps George Bush's own contribution to the development of presidential power will be to show that it is unreasonable for the citizenry, the media, and the Congress to expect a president to exercise policy leadership within a Madisonian framework designed to fragment power across separate institutions. In this sense, his presidency already represents a major departure from the governing approach of Ronald Reagan.

Administrative Strategies and Presidential Power

Reagan's use of prerogative powers suggests a strategic direction for future presidents. In the absence of a centralized legislative branch and the coherent political parties needed to build governing coalitions, presidents may want to employ an administrative strategy that uses a centralized scheme for presidential appointments, budget reconciliation, administrative clearance, and executive orders. These new sources of presidential power may help presidents meet the expectations of both the citizenry and the media, and help presidents to translate their campaign promises into concrete public policy. In this way, they will be better able to meet the requirements of the plebiscitary presidency.

Yet the Reagan strategy ran into serious difficulties in key policy areas, such as personnel management. While Interior Secretary James Watt and EPA Administrator Anne Gorsuch Burford pursued administrative strategies that helped to weaken the environmental and regulatory policies of the previous fifteen years, they eventually ran into opposition from Congress and environmental groups. In fact, the backlash was so great in response to Watt's and Burford's conservative environmental policies, to their abrasive styles of management, and to their lack of environmental experience that they were ultimately driven from office. In the end, the environmental movement received a major infusion of support and attention in response to the Reagan environmental policies.[80] Ironically, while Reagan's political appointees enabled him to turn back environmental regulations, over the long term these same appointments undermined his administrative strategy. As Richard Waterman concludes, "The case of the Reagan administration and the Environmental Protection Agency suggests that the administrative presidency strategy can be an effective means of promoting presidential influence, but not if implemented in the heavy-handed fashion of Burford and her team."[81] Presidents would be well advised to stress conciliation rather than confrontation in dealing with the federal bureaucracy. As the early Bush presidency has shown, cooperation, teamwork, and loyalty may well be better strategies if presidents want the long-term policy support of their executive branch appointments, Congress, and the media. The Reagan approach also suggests that future presidents should pay greater attention to the backgrounds and training of potential appointees to insure that individuals with the necessary expertise are appointed to the federal bureaucracy. A country purporting to be devoted to the republican form deserves, at least, that expertise.

In sum, the Reagan administrative strategy was a serious departure from the administrative approaches of previous presidents. His concerted effort to establish, from the beginning of his first term, top-down presidential control over the entire federal bureaucracy was unprecedented. The lesson for future presidents is that such an approach may well be an important source of presidential power in a highly fragmented political system. Yet such an approach is also fraught with risks and uncertainties. In the end, the Reagan experience seems to suggest that future presidents would be well advised to pursue an administrative strategy that emphasizes budgetary reform and centralization while also pursuing a coherent legislative strategy. Presidents might also want to listen to the admonition of political scientist Peri Arnold:

The plain fact is that no modern president has fully managed the executive branch. . . . It becomes clear that the managerial conception of the presidency is untenable. It places impossible obligations on presidents. It also raises public expectations about presidential performance that cannot be met. The managerial presidency then becomes a trap, offering increased capacity and influence to presidents but creating even greater expectations about presidential performance.[82]

Scholars of the presidency should also heed Arnold's warning. To the extent that we continue to raise expectations of presidential performance through various schemes to enlarge presidential power, we are merely reinforcing the impossible task that awaits any occupant of the Oval Office. Regardless of the administrative strategy that might be employed, no president can be expected to fully control the executive bureaucracy that characterizes a fragmented Madisonian system. Schemes designed to increase presidential control over the executive branch may well threaten democracy and accountability. The Reagan and Nixon cases make clear that there must be appropriate checks on presidents who attempt to accumulate power at the expense of the Congress, the Court, and the American people.

For political scientists, the study of various presidential administrative strategies may not move us any closer to developing a coherent theory of presidential power, but it will at least help us grapple with how various presidents have discovered new sources of presidential power in the mature modern era. In considering these new presidential prerogative power sources, it is also important to study how presidents have interpreted their foreign policy responsibilities. Chapter 5 raises these issues in light of the Reagan and Bush foreign policy efforts and the development of the plebiscitary presidency.

Notes

1. Richard Nathan, *The Administrative Presidency* (New York: John Wiley and Sons, 1983), p. 7.

2. Gary King and Lyn Ragsdale, *The Elusive Executive: Discovering Statistical Patterns in the Presidency* (Washington, D.C.: Congressional Quarterly Press, 1988), p. 25.

3. Francis Rourke, "Presidentializing the Bureaucracy." Paper prepared for delivery at the Annual Meeting of the American Political Science Association, Chicago, Illinois, September 3-6, 1987.

4. See Lester G. Seligman and Cary R. Covington, *The Coalitional Presidency* (Chicago: Richard D. Irwin, 1989).

5. John Hart, *The Presidential Branch* (Elmsford, New York: Pergamon, 1987), p. 24.

6. Hart, 1987, p. 25.

7. Hart, 1987, p. 26, and President's Committee on Administrative Management, *Administrative Management in the Government of the United States* (Washington, D.C.: U.S. Government Printing Office, 1937), p. 3.

8. Hart, 1987, p. 3.

9. James W. Fesler, "The Brownlow Committee Fifty Years Later," *Public Administration Review*, July/August 1987, Volume 47, Number 4, p. 292.

10. Hart, 1987, p. 29.

11. George C. Edwards III and Stephen J. Wayne, *Presidential Leadership: Politics and Policy Making*, 2nd ed. (New York: St. Martin's Press, 1990), p. 9.

12. King and Ragsdale, 1988, p. 24.

13. King and Ragsdale, 1988, p. 24.

14. See Theodore J. Lowi, *The Personal President: Power Invested and Promise Unfulfilled* (Ithaca: Cornell University Press, 1985) and *The End of Liberalism: The Second Republic of the United States*, 2nd ed. (New York: Norton, 1979).

15. See Richard Nathan, *The Administrative Presidency* (New York: John Wiley and Sons, 1983a) and Richard W. Waterman, *Presidential Influence and the Administrative State* (Knoxville: University of Tennessee Press, 1989) for detailed discussions of the Nixon centralized administrative strategy.

16. Nathan, 1983a, p. vii.

17. Richard Nathan, "The Reagan Presidency in Domestic Affairs," in Fred I. Greenstein, ed., *The Reagan Presidency: An Early Assessment* (Baltimore: Johns Hopkins University Press, 1983), p. 12.

18. James Pfiffner, "Introduction: The Presidency in Transition," in James Pfiffner and R. Gordon Hoxie, eds., *The Presidency in Transition*, Volume VI, Number 1 (New York: Center for the Study of the Presidency Proceedings, 1989), p. 4.

19. G. Calvin Mackenzie, "The Paradox of Presidential Personnel Management," in Hugh Heclo and Lester M. Salamon, eds., *The Illusion of Presidential Government* (Boulder, Colorado: Westview Press, 1981).

20. Seligman and Covington, 1989, pp. 115-116.

21. Rourke, 1987, p. 12.

22. See James Pfiffner, *The Strategic Presidency* (Homewood, Illinois: Dorsey, 1987) and Pfiffner, 1989, p. 4.

23. Pfiffner, 1989, pp. 4-5.

24. Terry M. Moe, "The Politicized Presidency," in John E. Chubb and Paul E. Peterson, eds., *The New Direction in American Politics* (Washington, D.C.: Brookings Institution, 1985), p. 260.

25. Robert Williams, "The President and the Executive Branch," in Malcolm T. Shaw, ed., *The Modern Presidency: From Roosevelt to Reagan* (New York: Harper and Row, 1987), p. 148.

26. Peter M. Benda and Charles H. Levine, "Reagan and the Bureaucracy: The Bequest, the Promise, and the Legacy," in Charles O. Jones, ed., *The Reagan Legacy: Promise and Performance* (Chatham, New Jersey: Chatham House Publishers, 1988), p. 107.

27. Bradley H. Patterson, Jr., *The Ring of Power* (New York: Basic Books, 1988), p. 108.

28. Moe, 1985, p. 260.

29. Benda and Levine, 1988, p. 108.

30. Mackenzie is quoted in Nathan, 1983a, p. 74.

31. See, for example, Michael Harrington, *The New American Poverty* (Chicago: Henry Holt, 1984); Fred Block, Richard Cloward, Barbara Ehrenreich, and Frances Fox Piven, eds., *The Mean Season* (New York: Pantheon, 1988); Richard Cloward and Frances Fox Piven, *The New Class War* (New York: Pantheon, 1985); and Michael Katz, *The Undeserving Poor* (New York: Pantheon, 1989).

32. Nathan, 1983a, p. 69.

33. Nathan, 1983a, p. 76.

34. Lester M. Salamon and Michael S. Lund, "Governing in the Reagan Era: An Overview," in Salamon and Lund, eds., *The Reagan Presidency and the Governing of America* (Washington, D.C.: The Urban Institute Press, 1985), p. 18.

35. Reagan is quoted in Julie Kosterlitz and W. John Moore, "Saving the Welfare State," *National Journal*, May 14, 1988, No. 20, p. 1276.

36. Salamon and Lund, 1985, p. 7.

37. Nathan, 1983a, p. 52.

38. Allen Schick, *Reconciliation and the Congressional Budget Process* (Washington, D.C.: American Enterprise Institute, 1981), p. 1.

39. For a partisan interpretation of his role, see David Stockman, *The Triumph of Politics* (New York: Harper and Row), 1986.

40. Salamon and Lund, 1985, p. 7.

41. Richard W. Waterman, *Presidential Influence and the Administrative State* (Knoxville: University of Tennessee Press, 1989), p. 39.

42. Waterman, 1989, pp. 38-39.

43. George C. Edwards III, "Preface: Presidential Policy Making," in George C. Edwards III, Steven A. Shull, and Norman Thomas, eds., *The Presidency and Public Policy Making* (Pittsburgh: University of Pittsburgh Press, 1985), p. xix.

44. William F. West and Joseph Cooper, "The Rise of Administrative Clearance," in Edwards, Shull, and Thomas, eds., 1985, p. 193.

45. Robert DiClerico, *The American President*, 3rd ed. (Englewood Cliffs, New Jersey: Prentice Hall, 1990), p. 176.

46. Ryan M. Barilleaux, *The Post-Modern Presidency* (New York: Praeger Press, 1988), pp. 86-87.

47. Martin Anderson, *Revolution* (New York: Harcourt Brace Jovanovich, 1988), pp. 56-57.

48. Reagan is quoted in Shirley Anne Warshaw, "Cabinet Government in the Modern Presidency," in Pfiffner and Hoxie, eds., 1989, p. 143.

49. Warshaw, 1989, p. 143.

50. Pfiffner, 1989, p. 12.

51. Pfiffner, 1989, p. 11.

52. Stephen Hess, *Organizing the Presidency*, 2nd ed. (Washington, D.C.: Brookings Institution, 1988), p. 140.

53. Anderson, 1988, p. 224.

54. Anderson, 1988, p. 225.

55. John Hart, "The President and his Staff," in Malcom T. Shaw, ed., *The Modern Presidency: From Roosevelt to Reagan* (New York: Harper and Row, 1987), p. 160.

56. For a thorough discussion and comparison of Jimmy Carter's and Ronald Reagan's administrative styles, see Colin Campbell, S.J., *Managing the Presidency: Carter, Reagan, and the Search for Executive Harmony* (Pittsburgh: University of Pittsburgh Press, 1986).

57. Ben W. Heineman, "Some Rules of the Game: Prescription for Organizing the Domestic Presidency," in Pfiffner and Hoxie, eds., 1989, p. 47.

58. Anderson, 1988, p. 295.

59. For a full discussion of such events, see Mark Hertsgaard, *On Bended Knee: The Press and the Reagan Presidency* (New York: Farrar, Straus, and Giroux, 1988).

60. Hess, 1988, p. 145.

61. George C. Edwards III, "Nowhere to Go and No Way to Get There: Congressional Relations in the Early Bush Administration," *The Political Science Teacher* Summer 1989, Volume 2, Number 3, p. 3.

62. See George C. Edwards III, *At the Margins: Presidential Leadership of Congress* (New Haven: Yale University Press, 1989) and Jon R. Bond and Richard Fleisher, *The President in the Legislative Arena* (Chicago: University of Chicago Press, 1990) for thoughtful empirical analyses of this hypothesis.

63. Edwards, 1989, p. 2.

64. James P. Pfiffner, "Establishing the Bush Presidency," *Public Administration Review* January/February 1990, Volume 50, p. 64.

65. Pfiffner, 1990, p. 71.

66. G. Calvin Mackenzie, "Issues and Problems in the Staffing of New Administrations," *The Political Science Teacher* Summer 1989, Volume 2, Number 3, p. 6.

67. Mackenzie, 1989, p. 6.

68. Pfiffner, 1990, p. 69.

69. Michael Duffy, "Mr. Consensus," *Time* August 21, 1989, pp. 18-19.

70. Pfiffner, 1990, p. 67.

71. Duffy, 1989, pp. 18-19.

72. See Gerald F. Seib, "Bush's Appointments Mark Him as a Man of the Establishment," *Wall Street Journal* December 14, 1988, p. 1.

73. Burt Solomon, "A Tangle of Old Relationships," *National Journal* September 30, 1989, Volume 26, p. 2418.

74. W. John Moore, "Hands Off," *National Journal* July 1, 1989, p. 1678.

75. See Allan R. Gold, "Series of Bush Appointments Worries Environmentalists," *New York Times* October 29, 1989 and John B. Oakes, "Bush Nominates Watt II," *New York Times*, November 8, 1989.

76. Dan Goodgame, "Big Bad John Sununu," *Time* May 21, 1990, p. 25.

77. See Andrew Rosenthal, "Sununu Says Bush 'Ad-Libbed' Comment on Credit Card Rates," *New York Times* November 23, 1991, p. A1.

78. Pfiffner, 1990, pp. 66-67.

79. R. W. Apple, "Sununu Tells How and Why He Pushed Souter for Court," *New York Times* July 25, 1990, p. A12.

80. Waterman, 1989, p. 134.

81. Waterman, 1989, pp. 142-143.

82. Peri E. Arnold, *Making the Managerial Presidency* (Princeton, New Jersey: Princeton University Press, 1986), pp. 361-362.

5

The Plebiscitary Presidency and American Foreign Policy in the Reagan and Bush Eras

"I will not, as commander-in-chief, ever put somebody into a military situation that we do not win—ever. And there's not going to be any long drawn-out agony of Vietnam."[1] Thus spoke President George Bush to a group of reporters at a CNN press conference on November 15, 1990, in response to the Persian Gulf crisis. Not surprisingly, the president's statement makes no reference to the role of Congress in committing American troops to combat. Despite the congressional reforms of the 1970s and 1980s designed to limit presidential aggrandizement of power in foreign policy, presidents have continually asserted their foreign policy prerogatives in military affairs. What have been the consequences of these congressional reforms for the roles of the president and Congress in the foreign policy process? What are the values and goals that have underlaid American foreign policy in the Reagan and Bush eras? Who should have the last say in directing American foreign policy and in committing American forces overseas? What is the relationship between presidential activity in foreign affairs and the plebiscitary presidency? Why do presidents turn to foreign policy concerns in an effort to bolster their public opinion ratings?

This chapter addresses these issues, within the context of an institutional and structural approach to presidential power,[2] by examining specific cases from the Reagan and Bush presidencies, including the 1983 invasion of Grenada, the 1983 bombing of a marine barracks in Lebanon, the 1987 Iran-Contra affair, the 1989 invasion of Panama, and the 1991 Persian Gulf war. This institutional and structural analysis approaches the role of the president in foreign policy in the more conventional political science sense by examining the balance of power between the president and Congress in American foreign policy during the Reagan and Bush eras. But to understand the sources of presidential foreign policy power, it is not enough to merely examine the constitutional framework. Attention must also be devoted to the underlying values and goals of American foreign policy and the role of the president in fostering such values around the world. In this sense, broader questions growing out of the normal operation of our liberal democracy push the more conventional institutional approach in a radical direction.

Several developments have strengthened executive dominance in foreign policy, especially in covert activities and military action. These include a changing world order that has challenged the U.S. ability to control events around the globe, the incentives of a plebiscitary presidency, congressional acquiescence in foreign affairs, and judicial tolerance for an expansive interpretation of presidential power. The Reagan and Bush approaches to foreign policy, their expansive views of executive foreign policy powers, and their adherence to the values associated with American exceptionalism provide a rich arena for evaluating such concerns. Their determination to establish Pax Americana around the globe has been demonstrated by attacking the so-called enemies of democracy and encouraging a world democratic vision characterized by the adherence to the American way: "law, representative government, human rights, a free-trade capitalist economy."[3]

Pax Americana and Presidential Power

Of all government actors, the president is viewed as being best situated, symbolically and strategically, to promote American interests throughout the world. Such interests have generally been related to the values associated with American exceptionalism. Political scientist Phil Williams has concluded that "the modern presidency is perhaps above all else a foreign policy presidency."[4]

Williams's assertion has certainly been true in the Reagan and Bush presidencies. Both administrations have failed to engender much critical self-reflection on the ideas at the foundation of American foreign policy. Indeed, these two presidents have appealed to a mindless patriotism and a "proud renunciation of the adversary culture"[5] in promoting American values around the world. The Reagan administration assumed power with a belief that American values had been increasingly threatened throughout the world. Ronald Reagan attempted to establish his foreign policy leadership in three ways: to contain the "Evil Empire" and adversary, the Soviet Union; to "reinvigorate U.S. alliances and foster support for American interests and goals;" and to impose American hegemony among Third World nations.[6] Both Reagan and Bush have attempted to restore the United States to a globally dominant position in ideological, economic, political and military spheres.[7] As William Pfaff suggests, "The unspoken but unmistakable assumption behind all of this was that the world would be a safe place for America only when the world was made very much like America. The corollary assumptions—that to make it so was possible and a reasonable goal of foreign policy—derived from the breathtaking conviction that people everywhere shared the fundamental ambitions and values of Americans."[8] Of all the actors in the American political system, the president is best situated to meet these challenges and to address these goals. Presidential scholar Thomas Cronin has written that the president "must convey in simple, uncluttered ways a sense of direction that will provide hope for Americans who want, above all else, a strong leader to lead."[9] Cronin's observation is particularly germane as we consider the role assumed by the president in foreign affairs. For a full understanding of why the President has been associated with strong leadership in American foreign policy and how that leadership has reinforced the plebiscitary presidency, we must examine the constitutional conflict between the president and Congress for controlling American foreign policy.

The Constitutional Context

Part of the problem facing scholars, politicians, and citizens as they attempt to ascertain the precise roles that Congress and the president should play in foreign affairs is rooted in the Constitution's comparatively vague statements regarding foreign policy. Both the Constitution and *The Federalist* fail to define executive power or to even list executive responsibilities clearly. As a result, it is difficult to ascertain the framers' intent. What this has meant in practice is that presidents have asserted themselves in the foreign policy vacuum created by the Constitution. Over the years, presidents have assumed that those powers not reserved expressly to the legislature can be exercised by the executive.[10]

When the constitutional framers mandated the president to be commander in chief of the armed forces and empowered Congress to appropriate money and declare war, they set the framework for extended conflict between the president and Congress in the foreign policy arena. According to constitutional historian Edward S. Corwin, the Constitution is "an invitation to struggle for the privilege of directing

American foreign policy."[11] Particularly in the areas of war-making and treaty-making powers, Congress and the president were afforded joint possession.

Through the years, however, the presidency has accumulated more foreign policy powers, especially in the Reagan and Bush eras. There are several reasons for this development. The president directs secret diplomatic negotiations and generally controls foreign affairs information. Given the unwieldy size of Congress, it is the president who must make the swift foreign policy decisions in a time of emergency. As commander in chief of the armed forces, the president can immediately order the armed forces into action.

This chapter argues that through the years, presidents have assumed considerable foreign policymaking powers at the expense of Congress and the citizenry, powers that threaten democratic accountability and the principles of representative government. In recent years, Congress has, in effect, acquiesced in the face of presidential aggrandizement of foreign policy powers. The imperial presidency concept needs revision in light of these recent developments. What ultimately matters, then, is not the intention of the constitutional framers but rather the consequences of their decisions for how foreign policy is conducted today. But to fully understand those consequences, it is first necessary to summarize what they did—and did not do—in terms of presidential power.

The powers conferred to Congress are fairly specific, whereas those given to the president are detailed within various roles assigned by the Constitution, particularly the role as commander in chief. Unlike the English monarch, the president was not awarded constitutional powers to commit the United States to war. What the framers did, however, was to vest Congress with the power to "declare" war rather than to "make" war as was originally suggested. In so doing, they provided the president with the power to respond militarily to sudden attacks. Article I, section 8, affords Congress the common defense and war declaration powers. Article II, section 2, allows presidents to appoint ambassadors with the advice and consent of the Senate, to be commander in chief of the armed forces, and to make treaties with the advice and consent of the Senate, as long as two-thirds of those senators present concur.[12] While these are powers expressly reserved for the president, they are awarded within the context of specific congressional limitations. This is more evidence that the framers wanted to limit presidential powers in foreign affairs. *The Federalist* and the Convention debates also provide clear evidence that key framers had serious concerns about giving the executive too much foreign policy power. In *Federalist #75*, Hamilton, who has traditionally been associated with those arguing for strong executive powers, rejects a strong executive in foreign affairs, largely because of his distrust of human nature: "The history of human conduct does not warrant that exalted opinion of human virtue which would make it wise in a nation to commit interests of so delicate and momentous a kind as those which concern its intercourse with the rest of the world to the sole disposal of a magistrate, created and circumstanced, as would be a president of the United States."[13] Likewise, Madison strongly rejects the notion that the executive should have the primary authority to declare war:

> In no part of the constitution is more wisdom to be found, than in the clause which confides the question of war or peace in the legislature, and not to the executive department. . . . War is in fact the true nurse of executive aggrandizement. . . . The strongest passions and most dangerous weaknesses of the human breast; ambition, avarice, vanity, the honorable or venial love of fame, are all in conspiracy against the desire and duty of peace. Hence it has grown into an axiom that the executive is the department of power most distinguished by its propensity to war; hence it is the practice of all states, in proportion as they are free, to disarm this propensity of its influence.[14]

To Madison, then, the power to declare war is a legislative act "and precisely because in carrying on war the executive is not executing law, its power in war should be construed narrowly. The executive has indeed a propensity to war, but this must be kept in check."[16]

In the end, the framers rejected the idea of presidential control over American foreign policy. Instead, they believed that foreign affairs powers should be shared between the executive and legislative branches. The framers would undoubtedly be surprised that the executive has played such a dominant role in foreign policy concerns since World War II. The expanding role of the executive can be traced to several arguments that have been consistently made on behalf of extending presidential power in foreign affairs.

One set of arguments emanates from the notion of unity, the belief that a single individual can better manage the foreign policy process than can hundreds of congressional members representing competing districts and states. A second argument is rooted in secrecy, the sense that the president is better equipped to handle covert activities than the diffuse Congress. A third suggests that because the executive has greater access to foreign policy information and expertise, the president should play a more active role than the legislature. Finally, proponents of greater executive power suggest "that the formulation and conduct of foreign policy would be executed more efficiently under White House, rather than congressional, control."[16]   This argument is based on the belief that Congress is a cumbersome, fragmented, and disjointed policymaking body. In international affairs, the president almost always has the upper hand because of his prestige, his role as commander in chief, and his prominent position in the minds of the citizenry and their belief that he can best promote American values throughout the world. The advent of the Cold War and the nuclear threat have also enhanced presidential power.

The Supreme Court has also played an important role in the allotment of foreign policy power. With its decision in the 1936 Curtiss-Wright case, the Supreme Court lent support for executive aggrandizement of power in the foreign policy arena. Writing for the majority, Justice George Sutherland stated that the authority in foreign affairs was essentially an executive power, which he explained as "the very delicate, plenary and exclusive power of the President as the sole organ of the federal government in the field of international relations—a power which does not require as a basis for its exercise, an act of Congress."[17] Those calling for greater executive prerogative power in foreign policy have turned to the Curtiss-Wright decision for support.

From the vantage point of members of Congress, foreign policy is not a politically advantageous issue.[18]   Foreign policy concerns are simply not appreciated by constituents and as a result, congressional members lack the incentive to become involved in international affairs. One member of the Senate Foreign Relations Committee said: "It's a political liability. . . . You have no constituency. In my reelection campaign last fall, the main thing they used against me was that because of my interest in foreign relations, I was more interested in what happened to the people of Abyssinia and Afghanistan than in what happened to the good people of my state."[19] Others have at least acknowledged that Congress can play a role in foreign policy, but that role is almost always at the margin. Representative Lee Hamilton (D-Indiana), the ranking Democrat on foreign affairs, said: "We can modify, we can alter.   But the fundamental policy remains the President's policy."[20]

It would be a facile generalization to suggest that Congress plays a minimal role in the foreign policy process without providing more concrete examples for such a claim. In fact, evidence suggests that in recent years, Congress has become more assertive in foreign affairs, including attempts to recover hostages, foreign aid, foreign intelligence and covert activities, arms sales, and intervention in rebel movements against foreign governments.[21] Congressional scholar Thomas Mann concludes that Congress began to reassert itself in foreign affairs during the late 1960s, as the American people began to doubt the Vietnam

War.[22] During the Reagan years, Congress took the lead in U.S. policy toward South Africa and imposed economic sanctions over the president's veto. Congress also asserted itself in Central American policy by blocking the Reagan administration's fervent military support for the Nicaraguan Contras.[23] Early in the Bush administration Congress claimed a victory of sorts when it passed legislation guaranteeing that Chinese students could stay in the United States. Representative Stephen Solarz (D-New York) said: "That demonstrated there were strong feelings in Congress and that [members] were prepared to buck the President."[24] But President Bush ultimately proved victorious as the Senate was unable to override his veto, a powerful institutional mechanism used quite often and effectively during the first three years of the Bush presidency.

The record suggests that in response to a more aggressive executive in foreign policy, Congress has institutionalized procedures to allow for a much more active oversight role in foreign policy and defense concerns, especially in challenging the president's ability to wage an undeclared war. A central issue is the circumstances under which Congress chooses to exercise or abdicate the important foreign policy responsibilities that the framers intended for the legislative branch. Before looking at the role of Congress in specific foreign policy cases during the Reagan and Bush years, it is first necessary to outline the various congressional reforms of the 1970s and 1980s that were designed to respond to the perceived excessive executive aggrandizement of power in foreign affairs.

The Congressional Foreign Policy Reforms of the 1970s and 1980s

In response to the perception that the executive branch had accumulated far too much foreign policy power in the Vietnam era, Congress enacted several reforms in an effort to expand its influence over foreign policy. Congress developed its own foreign affairs bureaucracy through staff expansion and the hiring of personnel with foreign policy interests and expertise. In addition, the legislature sought to control foreign policy appropriations by limiting the amount of U.S. aid to other countries. Congress has also demanded routine access to intelligence information. The executive branch can no longer withhold classified information and expect Congress to acquiesce. Congressional members now have more freedom to stake out independent positions on foreign policy concerns in the absence of a strong seniority and party discipline system. The Vietnam era suggests that congressional opposition to a divisive war is an opportunity for the media attention and popular recognition that all members of Congress seek. In recent years we have seen greater congressional travel abroad, which has fostered instant foreign policy expertise and given members of Congress the opportunity to negotiate directly with foreign leaders. All of these factors have contributed to a more assertive Congress in foreign affairs.[25] Congress also implemented a number of important procedural mechanisms that allow for the legislature to play a much more active role in the foreign policy process.

The War Powers Resolution of 1973

In late 1973 Congress adopted the War Powers Resolution, overriding President Nixon's veto with a more than two-thirds majority. The resolution's purpose was to regulate the conduct of the executive in committing American troops to military action without congressional approval. Under the War Powers Resolution, the president must meet the following conditions:

1. The action must be reported and detailed to Congress within forty-eight hours.
2. The action must be ended within sixty days and American forces withdrawn within ninety days unless Congress extends the combat commitment.
3. A congressional resolution can end the combat commitment at any time; this resolution is not subject to a presidential veto.

What have been the consequences of the resolution for the interaction between the president and Congress in international affairs? Richard Rose points out that the resolution provides evidence to support his claim that "when Congress enacts laws to restrain the President's room for maneuver in the international system, it unintentionally illustrates the limited effectiveness of congressional action."[26] While the resolution was originally lauded as a mechanism for preventing U.S. involvement in another Vietnam situation, it has proved over time to be "a symbol of congressional insistence that Congress has the ultimate power to declare war coupled with acquiescence to the practical realities of the modern world."[27] The central problem is the vagueness of the statute and the opportunity it presents for presidents to interpret the law as they see fit. The Reagan and Bush presidencies provide evidence to support this claim. All presidents since Nixon have been opposed to the resolution, and all but Carter have questioned its constitutionality. At a minimum, presidents have viewed the resolution as limiting their ability to protect vital American interests around the world. None have been willing to comply with the resolution's dictates. Presidents have been willing to inform Congress before committing troops abroad but have thus far refused to invoke the resolution in an effort to avoid the sixty-day timetable. They have consistently argued that if they did adhere to the War Powers Resolution, they would "give Congress unconstitutional power over U.S. troops that properly rests with the President as commander in chief."[28] Ironically, presidents actually have more foreign policy powers as a result of the War Powers Resolution. As Barilleaux concludes, "They now possess an effective license to commit U.S. troops without congressional approval."[29] This is an important and powerful new presidential prerogative in the foreign policy arena. The resolution is also unworkable because it fails to take into account presidential and congressional interests in war-making decisions. According to Thomas Mann, it fails in a number of areas:

> Presidents insist on retaining the discretion to act quickly and decisively to protect American security interests; that ability is lost if legislative action can force troops to withdraw. Members of Congress want to be consulted by the president before military forces are deployed; they also want a practical means of terminating military actions whose costs outweigh their benefits. But the resolution provides neither the mechanism for consultation nor a politically feasible way for Congress to reverse the president's course in those rare instances when it might seek to do so.[30]

Congress deserves considerable blame for failing to force presidents to comply with the resolution and for avoiding ways to improve the quality of congressional involvement in military affairs. Daniel Paul Franklin argues that Congress has neglected enforcing the War Powers Resolution because it does not have an established system for facilitating consultation and because congressional members tend to be interested only in "acute foreign policy issues."[31] From Franklin's perspective, the resolution has satisfied the standard of congressional intent because "the original consultation provision was not worded strongly."[32] The central weakness of the War Powers Resolution is that it fails to take into account the likelihood that presidents will ignore its requirements. Congress could impeach a president, but that has only been seriously considered on two occasions in U.S. history.[33] Impeachment is not considered a viable option, although some called for it on various occasions in the Reagan presidency, largely in response to the Iran-Contra affair. Foreign policy cases involving American military action during the Reagan and Bush presidencies provide evidence to support the claim that the War Powers Resolution is an ineffective, unclear, and largely meaningless congressional attempt to control presidential war-making powers.

The Resolution in Practice

Lebanon.   In late summer 1983 President Reagan sent marine contingents to Lebanon to reinforce the multilateral force supporting President Gemayel's besieged government. In dispatching the marines on August 25, Reagan hoped to bring peace and stability to Lebanon and to reduce tensions in the Middle East. The president reported his action to Congress on August 24 so that he would be complying with the War Powers Resolution.[34] President Reagan met the requirement to report to Congress, but failed to mention the term "hostilities." Instead "the Administration argued that the American units would be carrying out a 'peace mission' as part of a multilateral force to strengthen a friendly government and should not be seen as potential combatants." The mission was defined in ways that would allow avoidance of the War Powers Resolution's dictates, most notably the sixty-day mechanism.[35]

Congress grew increasingly uncomfortable with the presence of the marines and began to question whether the situation would lead to "imminent" hostilities. As Crabb and Holt point out, "If it was, then under the War Powers Resolution they could stay no more than sixty days—in exceptional circumstances, ninety days—unless Congress declared war or passed a specific statutory authorization." In response, Congress passed the Lebanon Emergency Assistance Act of 1983, which mandated that the "President shall obtain statutory authorization . . . with respect to any substantial expansion in the number or role in Lebanon of United States Armed Forces." With this act, Congress was in essence saying that it accepted the president's "policy thus far but was uneasy over where it might lead."[36]

On August 29 the marines suffered their first casualties when two were killed and fourteen wounded by hostile mortar fire. U.S. warships retaliated by shelling artillery positions. President Reagan still refused to file the report required by the War Powers Resolution and offered the following rationale for not doing so: "Isolated or infrequent acts of violence [do not necessarily constitute] imminent involvement in hostilities."[37] This outbreak of combat in the Middle East led Congress to recognize that American involvement in Lebanon had changed from a peacekeeping role to "support for one side in a bitter civil war."[38] The congressional response led to long negotiations with the Reagan administration, ultimately resulting in a congressional resolution that authorized American marines to remain in Lebanon for eighteen more months. In signing the resolution, Reagan claimed that his differences with Congress were over "institutional prerogatives," but that these differences must remain secondary to insuring Congressional support for his Middle East policies. He also stressed executive authority in foreign policy, adding: "I do not and cannot cede any of the authority vested in me under the Constitution as President and as Commander in Chief of United States Armed Forces."[39]

American policy in Lebanon took a violent turn just three weeks later, when a truckful of explosives went through a barricade, collapsing a building and killing 241 sleeping marines. The rancorous public debate that followed led President Reagan to order the evacuation of the 1,400-marine contingent, more than one year short of the eighteen-month deadline. Senator Sam Nunn of Georgia, the ranking Democrat on the Armed Services Committee, posed this question: "It seems to me that we ought to go back to the drawing board and say, 'Mr. President, what are the marines doing there and under what terms would they be withdrawn?'" Senator Alan Cranston represented a majority view in Congress when he labeled the situation "a total mess." Cranston continued, "There is no clear way out. We cannot retreat under fire and if we were to declare war we wouldn't know who to declare war against."[40] As Nunn and Cranston's comments suggest, the central problem for the Reagan administration was that the American marine presence had been ill-defined from the outset. At first the marines were sent to support the Lebanese government, enhance the morale of the people, and prepare to aid police in the event of an evacuation by the Israeli, Syrian, and Palestinian forces. Prior to the October 23 attack, however, the Reagan administration claimed that the marines, supported by U.S. Navy ships, were protecting the Lebanese Army and challenging efforts by Syrian-backed Druse and Shiite factions to undermine the Lebanese Government.[41]

By almost all accounts, Reagan's handling of the entire affair was a disaster. In his comprehensive biography of Ronald Reagan, Lou Cannon offers a typical and sobering commentary on the Reagan administration's involvement in Lebanon:

> The story of the Reagan administration's involvement in Lebanon is a case study of foreign policy calamity. More than any other under-taking, the U.S. involvement in Lebanon demonstrates the naivete, ignorance and undisciplined internal conflict characteristic of the Reagan presidency. More than any other policy, Reagan's course of action in Lebanon displays his proclivity for splitting the difference between irreconcilable positions at the sacrifice of clarity—and in this case, of American lives. More than any other crisis, Lebanon illustrates the ambiguity of Reagan's presidential leadership.[42]

The case of Lebanon also reveals some of the problems associated with the War Powers Resolution. The fact that the legislation says nothing about the criteria for identifying when hostilities have actually begun affords presidents advantages in dealing with Congress. Congress had actually given its consent to keeping the marines in Lebanon. As a result, little could be said when terrorists attacked the marine barracks. In addition, the Lebanon debacle suggests that presidents should use U.S. forces massively, with the aim of total victory, if they desire a military solution that is consistent with the War Powers Resolution but does not involve Congress. This is hardly what the congressional authors of the resolution had in mind when it was created in 1973.[43] The situation in Grenada reveals some of the same concerns.

Grenada. Just two days after the marine barracks bombing in Lebanon, American marine attachments and army units invaded Grenada. President Reagan claimed that the purpose of the operation was "to protect our own citizens," referring to American medical students studying in Grenada, and to "help in the restoration of democratic institutions in Grenada" where "a brutal group of leftist thugs violently seized power."[44] U.S. officials feared that Prime Minister Maurice Bishop had established too many close ties with Cuba and the Soviet Union, and this was anathema to American foreign policy interests in the region. Subsequently, little evidence was provided to support such claims, and both Democrats and Republicans on the Senate Select Committee on Intelligence claimed that Cuban influence on Grenada was exaggerated.[45] The Reagan administration also voiced concern that Grenada could become another Iran, where Americans were held hostage for 244 days, or another Beirut, where the United States was powerless to prevent the terrorist killing of more than 200 marines.[46]

Congressional critics challenged the administration's invasion rationale and they questioned whether the purported danger faced by American medical students was a credible justification for the invasion. Representative Peter Kostmayer (D-Pennsylvania) said: "The administration has not demonstrated that their action was necessary, and they have not demonstrated, morally or ethically, that it was right. I haven't seen a single shred of evidence that American lives were in danger in Grenada."[47] But in the face of televised speech in which Reagan explained his reasons for the invasion to the American people and the resulting wave of patriotism sweeping the nation, congressional criticism became increasingly muted. Some members of Congress were concerned that the administration largely excluded congressional leaders from the planning and decisionmaking leading up to the October 25 invasion.[48] Most criticism centered on Reagan's refusal to adhere to the dictates of the War Powers Resolution rather than challenge the invasion itself.

In an effort to partially comply with the War Powers Resolution, the president formally notified congressional leaders that American troops had begun landing in Grenada. Reagan failed, however, to report that the troops had been sent "into hostilities or into situations where imminent involvement in hostilities is clearly indicated by the circumstances," as required by the resolution.[49] Democrats in Congress called for the president to honor the resolution by agreeing to the sixty-day timetable and by including a formal statement to that effect in a letter to Congress. Reagan refused to do so and thus circumvented the role that Congress might have played in the Grenadan military commitment. The resolution had virtually no impact on the decision to invade.

In sum, despite the existence of the War Powers Resolution, Congress played a minimal role in the invasion of Grenada. There was mild criticism of the Reagan administration decision, but this soon dissipated in the face of American military resolve, "victory," and patriotic sentiment. It is interesting to note, that the Reagan administration's decision to restrict news coverage in the first days of the invasion prompted little criticism from Congress. Most of the criticism emanated from the press itself, a phenomena to be replayed again during the 1991 Persian Gulf war. For Ronald Reagan and his supporters, the invasion of Grenada successfully deflected public, congressional, and media attention from the Beirut disaster by tapping into the values and symbols long associated with American imperialistic foreign policy. Once again, a president revelled in the admiration of the American people as he took decisive action to supposedly protect American lives and interests in Grenada. Reagan's public opinion ratings increased noticeably, thus providing him with good reason to emphasize foreign policy concerns as he attempted to meet the requirements of the plebiscitary presidency (see Figure 3.1). A variation on the same theme was also seen in President Reagan's decision to bomb Libya.

Libya. In response to increased terrorist activity on the part of Libya, Ronald Reagan approved a plan by the Joint Chiefs of Staff for surgical bombing strikes against Libya. The plan was carried out on April 14, 1986, when American air strikes near Tripoli and Benghazi were justified by the president as a "single engagement in a long battle against terrorism."[50] Reagan received an immediate boost in public opinion polls as the American people rallied around his decision to punish the villain Qaddafi (see Figure 3.1). A series of incidents had heightened tensions between the Reagan administration and Qaddafi during the 1980s. In August 1981, Qaddafi challenged U.S. naval units in the Mediterranean that had sailed through the Gulf of Sidra because he claimed they were Libyan waters, not international waters as asserted by the United States. Two Libyan jets were shot down by the American units because their approach was deemed hostile. Reagan made no report on this incident to Congress, most likely because it was over quickly and there was no damage to U.S. ships or planes.[51]

A larger clash between U.S. and Libyan forces in and over the Gulf of Sidra occurred in March 1986. Libya attacked U.S. planes from shore installations and "the United States responded with air-to-surface missiles, which temporarily disabled the Libyan radar." Libyan patrol boats were also attacked by U.S. ships. Reagan informed Congress of the incident "in accordance with my desire that the Congress be informed on this matter."[52] Yet he failed to even mention the War Powers Resolution, and there is little evidence that he consulted congressional leaders before or during the clash.

The April 1986 bombings were in direct response to the April 5, 1986, bombing of a West Berlin discotheque frequented by American soldiers. One of the soldiers and a Turkish woman were killed and 230 were wounded. Soon after the bombings, American intelligence claimed that "they had established Libyan complicity in the West Berlin incident from intercepted communications."[53] In reporting this action to Congress, Reagan cited the War Powers Resolution.

But after the attack, and despite apparent strong public support for the president's action, some members of Congress challenged the Reagan administration's expansive interpretation of presidential power to act in "self-defense" against terrorism. Reagan had used military power against Libya twice within a month and failed to seek extensive advice or approval from Congress in either case. Dante B. Fascell (D-Florida), chairman of the House Foreign Affairs Committee, claimed that Reagan had developed "a new way of going to war which totally bypasses the Constitution."[54] He also lamented the administration's unwillingness to adhere to the War Powers Resolution by "waltzing around the act [and complying with it] only when it suits them."[55]

Other members of Congress drew a very different conclusion from the Libyan case. They claimed that Reagan's tough response against terrorist activity provides credence to the administration's view that when responding to terrorist acts, the president needs greater freedom from congressional oversight in military affairs. A group of Republicans from both houses of Congress introduced legislation that would exempt "from the constraints of the War Powers Act a decision by the President to respond to a terrorist act or threat of terrorism with 'deadly force.'" Senator Bob Dole, the Senate majority leader at the time and one of the bill's sponsors, justified his support for the measure by arguing that its purpose was "to avoid these pointless debates about whether consultations three hours in advance is enough or whether you need four or five hours or whatever."[56]

The legislation failed to get the bipartisan support needed for approval. But the very fact that it was introduced and gained some support from members in both houses suggests that Congress itself is uneasy with enforcing the War Powers Resolution in the face of presidential assertions of executive prerogative in foreign affairs. The Bush administration's invasion of Panama in 1989 illustrates this point even more dramatically.

Panama. "We invaded Panama after the death of the marine, the brutalizing, really obscene torture of the navy lieutenant, and the threat of sexual abuse and the terror inflicted on that navy lieutenant's wife; the declaration of war by Noriega; the fact that our people weren't sure that we could guarantee the safety of Americans there." George Bush offered that explanation in a press conference following the December 20, 1989, invasion of Panama. He might also have said that his goal was to install a government that would be more supportive of the U.S. conception of democracy than the Noriega regime had been in recent years.[57] Bush claimed later that he "took this action only after reaching the conclusion that every other avenue was closed."[58] There is little doubt, too, that Bush felt pressure to resolve the Noriega situation after the administration's failed October 3 coup.[59]

How did the Bush administration reach its decision to invade Panama? Many of the post-invasion reports stressed President Bush's penchant for secrecy in an effort to protect the element of surprise. As a result, few officials outside Bush's cabinet were informed that such an invasion would take place until mere hours before the invasion. There was little chance, then, that Congress might be able to challenge Bush's plan or even offer an alternative response to the Panamanian situation.[60]

The response of Congress to the invasion and the ultimate capture of Manuel Noriega was overwhelmingly positive.[61] Prior to the invasion, congressional members had openly ridiculed the administration for its inept handling of the failed October 3 coup. House Speaker Tom Foley (D-Washington) offered this patriotic sentiment: "Under the circumstances, the decision is justified. When there is the engagement of U.S. forces in the field, it behooves all of us to give that support."[62] Congressional opposition, muted as it was, took the form of challenging executive prerogative to initiate hostilities without appropriate congressional involvement. Representative Charles Rangel (D-New York) said: "What is the purpose of the constitutional authority of the Congress to declare war if the president can do it unilaterally?"[63] Others expressed concern over the operation's efficiency, its duration, and its long-term consequences.[64]

The War Powers Resolution did little to affect the Bush administration's decision to invade. One student of Congress concluded that the Panamanian case provides plenty of support for the conclusion that the resolution is "a dead letter."[65] President Bush did notify the House and Senate leadership on December 22, some sixty hours after the invasion began. In addition, he telephoned top congressional leaders on December 19, several hours before the invasion, to notify them but not consult them, regarding his imminent action. Like his predecessors, Bush avoided invoking the procedural trigger of the War Powers Resolution. He never formally invoked the law and was thus able to avoid the sixty-day limit on troop involvement.[66] Congress played virtually no role in the decision to invade or in the invasion aftermath.

But the Panamanian case is disturbing for other reasons as well. Significant evidence suggests that the administration overstated Noriega's role as a drug smuggler. The prosecution in Miami has admitted that it has no hard evidence linking Noriega to drugs. Panama in the early 1990s has a narrowly based, oligarchic government that was sworn in on an American military base—hardly the "democratic" form hoped for by the administration. The Independent Commission of Inquiry on the U.S. Invasion of Panama also found that the Panama Canal was never really in danger. But perhaps most disturbing of all is the number of lives lost as a result of the American invasion. Basking in the glow of victory and the accompanying patriotism, the State Department's initial death counts for the operation were 314 Panamanian military fatalities, 202 Panamanian civilians and 23 U.S. troops. Television's "60 Minutes" ran a feature report that concluded that "as many as 4,000 Panamanian civilians had died in the conflict."[67] The Independent Commission's written report, published in early 1991, found that "from 1,000 to 4,000 Panamanians were killed, thousands more were wounded, and more than 20,000 found themselves homeless."[68] In the face of these casualties and the dire situation Panama confronts under the Endara government in the early 1990s, we might ask these questions: Why was Noriega reviled so much in 1989, but not in the early and mid-1980s when he was viewed as an important ally to the United States?[69] How can the invasion of Panama be justified, especially in light of the number of casualties reported by the Independent Commission? How could there possibly be such widespread support for this military action among the Congress and the mainstream press? To what extent could Congress have prevented the military action even if it chose to do so? The answer to the last question is that Congress probably could not have prevented the Bush adminis- tration from engaging in military activity unless it voted to cut off all funds for the military initiative. But Congress failed to do even that and instead exercised little meaningful opposition. In the case of Panama, the Bush administration used the War Powers Resolution to strengthen executive prerogative in the military arena. Even if Congress had insisted that President Bush comply with the resolution, the president would have ultimately had the power and authority to determine whether to invade and how long American troops would remain in a military commitment.

The Persian Gulf War. Most presidential scholars and journalists have identified the 1991 Persian Gulf war as a defining moment for the Bush presidency. The events leading up to the war and the war itself are of interest because they provide an opportunity to examine the role of America in a "new world order," the role of Congress in an incipient military action, the viability of the War Powers Resolution, the Bush administration's foreign policy style, and the patriotic response of the citizenry within the context of the plebiscitary presidency.

The Bush administration has had great difficulty in defining why the United States needed a military presence in the Persian Gulf. The administration gave a number of justifications for our involvement during the six months of U.S. deployments in the gulf:

1. "A mad dictator" who wants to control "the economic well-being of every country in the world.". . .
2. "Oil-lifeline threatened.". . .
3. "It is aggression." "Protecting freedom means standing up to aggression.". . .
4. "Iraq's aggression is not just a challenge to the security of Kuwait and the other gulf neighbors but to the better world we all hope to build in the wake of the Cold War. We're not talking simply about the price of gas. We are talking about the price of liberty.". . .
5. "It is the national security." "It is a world order that is threatened.". . .
6. "If you want to sum it up in one word, it's jobs.". . .
7. "Restore rulers to Kuwait.". . .
8. "Nuclear threat."[70]

When he was questioned by CNN interviewers on November 15, 1991, regarding his inability to clearly articulate his motivation for the American military presence in the Persian Gulf, Bush replied: "If I haven't done as clear a job as I might on explaining this, then I've got to do better in that regard, because I know in my heart of hearts that what we are doing is right."[71] President Bush's own lack of clarity did not prevent Congress and the mainstream American press from supporting the Persian Gulf military effort.

The role of Congress in the Persian Gulf crisis had been unclear since August 2, 1991, when President Bush sent 240,000 U.S. troops to Saudi Arabia, less than one week after Saddam Hussein's invasion of

Kuwait. Bush did consult briefly with congressional leaders before committing troops to Saudi Arabia and briefed a larger group of congressional members who had returned to Washington during the recess. Both the House and Senate passed October resolutions supporting Bush's policy of "relying on economic sanctions to coerce Iraq out of Kuwait and stationing troops in Saudi Arabia to deter an attack on that U.S. ally."[72] During September and October, a number of congressional members argued that Congress should invoke the War Powers Resolution in an effort to force Congress to take a stand in support of or in opposition to Bush's policy. But this was rejected by House and Senate leaders because they considered the resolution to be unworkable.[73] Senator Joseph Lieberman (D-Connecticut) offered a typical response: "I support what the President has done so far. If he decides to take military action, I don't expect him to call me up first. No President will ever fulfill the terms of the War Powers Act."[74]

The limited role played by Congress was reflected immediately after the November congressional elections. President Bush announced that he was increasing the number of U.S. forces to 400,000 and calling in reserve support. He did not consult Congress before taking either action. It was at that point that the president committed the United States to war. Despite opposition to military action from Secretary of State James Baker and Chairman of the Joint Chiefs of Staff Colin Powell, Bush was clearly gearing up for a protracted American military role in the Persian Gulf.[75]

When it became clear that he would win the support of Congress, Bush asked Congress to give him the authorization to go to war against Iraq if it did not leave Kuwait. The Senate voted 52-47 and the House 250-183 in support of a resolution to authorize the use of military force against Iraq. The Bush administration viewed the votes as congressional support for a military response against Iraq, but the divided vote revealed serious divisions in Congress and the American people over the wisdom of going to war. Most legal experts claimed that "despite the significance of Congress' action on the Persian Gulf, the constitutional debate over the power to wage war remains as unsettled as ever."[76] Congress played virtually no role in the president's decision to send 240,000 American soldiers to Saudi Arabia in August 1990 or in the decision to increase the number to 400,000 in early November. Congress should have and could have demanded the opportunity to participate in the troop deployment decisionmaking process. At this point, however, the president and his chief officials were unwilling to allow congressional members to exercise their constitutional prerogative and participate in any meaningful way. In testimony before the Senate Armed Services Committee, Secretary of Defense Dick Cheney argued that President Bush did not need authorization from Congress to launch a major military offensive into Kuwait. Bush received advice from Deputy Attorney General William Barr suggesting that the president had the constitutional authority to conduct military operations as the commander in chief of the armed forces, regardless of whether Congress passed a resolution of support.[77] Once again, a president had found a way to exercise executive prerogative in the face of an unclear constitutional context about the role of Congress and an unwillingness on the part of Congress to seek out more opportunities for a meaningful role in foreign affairs. The Persian Gulf war and the invasion of Panama provide evidence to support Berman and Jentleson's conclusion that George Bush "has strong and deep presidentialist inclinations and sees executive imperatives in the conduct of foreign affairs."[78]

The war itself and events since the war suggest that despite the outpouring of patriotic support for American troops in this country, our so-called victory in the Persian Gulf must be placed within the context of the tremendous loss of life in Iraq and Kuwait, the destruction of the environment, and the Kurdish uprising in the aftermath of the cease-fire. The Bush administration chose to do little for the fleeing Kurds and "the administration continued to speak of a new world order in the Middle East even as Iraqi helicopter gunships slaughtered thousands of Kurds."[79] Most importantly, Saddam Hussein remained in power. Throughout the war, the American people were subjected to military control of the press and press censorship that had not been seen in this century. In the end, the Bush administration had still not fully justified American involvement in the Middle East by identifying concrete goals, especially given the political and environmental instability, as well as the death and destruction, that was the result of the Persian Gulf war. Yet he and the American public basked in the glow of a "great victory," thus bolstering the president's popularity (see Figure 3.1) and reinforcing the central elements of the plebiscitary presidency.

Executive Power and Covert Actions: The Congressional Response

From an analysis of the War Powers Resolution, it is clear that President Reagan sought to reassert presidential prerogative in foreign affairs, as was illustrated by his ability to unilaterally deploy military force overseas with the invasion of Grenada and the bombing of Libya. The Reagan administration also embraced covert actions by greatly increasing the CIA's budget and personnel and by circumventing congressional scrutiny of intelligence operations.[80]

Presidents who wish to bypass Congress in order to achieve their foreign policy goals often turn to covert activities. The Nixon administration, in particular, embraced such actions in an effort to circumvent the will of Congress and the American people. In response, Congress passed a number of reforms, including the 1974 Hughes-Ryan amendment and the 1980 Intelligence Oversight Act, in an effort to reassert itself in the intelligence arena. The Iran-Contra affair offers an excellent opportunity to evaluate how well these reforms have worked in practice.

In response to American covert activities intended to prevent Salvador Allende from becoming president of Chile, Congress used the 1974 foreign aid bill to pass the Hughes-Ryan amendment. The amendment required that covert actions, which were distinguished from purely intelligence operations, conducted "by or on behalf of" the CIA must be reported to "the appropriate committees of the Congress."[81] It also prohibited the CIA from engaging in actions other than intelligence gathering unless the president "finds that each such operation is important to the national security of the United States and reports, in a timely fashion, a description and scope of such operation to the appropriate committees of the Congress." The Hughes-Ryan law "was the first law ever passed by Congress specifically calling for congressional oversight of intelligence activities."[82] It is also important because it places a time limit on the president's reporting on covert activities.

Congressional reforms of the intelligence process culminated in the 1980 Intelligence Oversight Act, which obligated the intelligence community to consult with Congress in every possible way when engaging in any "significant anticipated intelligence activity," including covert operations. This stiffened the consultative requirement significantly.[83] In return, Congress decreased the number of committees to which the president was required to report from eight to two.

With Executive Order 12333, signed into law on December 4, 1981, the Reagan administration completed the codification of the entire intelligence system. The Hughes-Ryan requirements no longer applied only to the CIA, but now to the entire intelligence community. The National Security Council was afforded greater prominence as "the highest Executive Branch entity that provides review of, guidance for and direction to the conduct of all national foreign intelligence, counterintelligence, and special activities, and attendant policies and programs." This language seems to award sweeping control to the entire NSC, not only to the president. Under the guidelines of the executive order, the responsibility for covert activities was given to the CIA and its director.[84]

These reforms had consequences for the Reagan administration's covert activities. As Theodore Draper points out, "The role of the

NSC's staff in the Iran-contra affairs raised the question whether the staff was part of the 'intelligence community' and thus came under the Hughes-Ryan legislation and other reporting requirements."[86]   The extent to which the congressional reforms and the Reagan executive order meant that covert activities were under greater congressional control can best be understood by examining the Iran-contra affair and broader questions of whether covert actions can be squared with democratic principles.

The Iran-Contra affair is revealing not only because it raises important questions regarding the goals of American foreign policy in Central America and executive authority in foreign policy but also because it displays the ineptness of Congress in challenging such goals and authority.   The congressional hearings devoted to the Iran-Contra scandal failed to explore the full range of transgressions associated with the Reagan administration's efforts to promote the Contra cause.   In the words of Yale Law professor Harold Koh, Congress lost a golden opportunity to evaluate the question: "Why does the President almost always seem to win in foreign affairs?"   Koh contends that had the Iran-Contra Committees considered this question, "they would have found the answer in a combination of three institutional factors: executive initiative, congressional acquiescence, and judicial tolerance."[86]

Soon after taking office, Ronald Reagan exercised executive initiative in his determination to undermine the Sandinista government in Nicaragua.   On April 1, 1981, the Reagan administration cut off all aid to the Nicaraguan government.   With this decision, "the possibility of any diplomatic solution to the U.S.-Nicaragua dispute during Reagan's term in office was probably doomed in the first three months of the administration."[87]   His policies can be placed within the broader context of his virulent anti-communism, his determination to promote American values throughout the world, and his willingness to attack so-called enemies of American capitalism and representative government.   The Reagan administration stepped up its anti-Sandinista activities as the Sandinistas promoted leftist policies and supported the leftist rebel movement in El Salvador.   Reagan's great fear was that the El Salvadoran rebels would gain control of the government and embrace leftist reforms that in Reagan's mind were associated with Soviet-style communism and would be inimical to American corporate interests.   Under the direction of William Casey, the CIA devised a covert operation designed "to stop the flow of arms from Nicaragua through Honduras to the guerrilla movement in El Salvador."[88]   Casey's plan resulted in a $19-million program to train and support the Contras, a group based in Honduras who desired to remove the Sandinistas from power.   Congress responded by passing the first Boland amendment as a part of the fiscal 1983 authorization bill. The amendment prohibited military activities in support of "any group or individual, not part of a country's armed forces, for the purpose of overthrowing the government of Nicaragua or provoking a military exchange between Nicaragua and Honduras."[89] This did little to prevent the Reagan administration from pursuing its efforts to undermine the Sandinista government.

In January 1984, CIA Director Casey displayed his contempt for the Sandinistas, for Congress, and for international law when American magnetic mines were placed in three Nicaraguan harbors. The mining was done in the utmost secrecy and attracted little immediate attention because the CIA encouraged the Contras to take credit for it. But an April 6 *Wall Street Journal* story revealed that the CIA, rather than the Contras, had been responsible for the minings. President Reagan had given his approval to the action, which resulted in damage to several ships, including a Soviet oil tanker. Donald Gregg, a thirty-year veteran of the CIA, later testified that the mining was designed "to sink a Soviet ship or any ship bringing military supplies to the Sandinista regime or to block a channel through which military supplies would have to pass." Congress was enraged by this contempt of the law; they were supposed to be informed prior to the implementation of any "important covert operation."[90] As Draper points out, "President Reagan let Casey take all the heat, as if the president had been an innocent bystander."[91]

The congressional response was the second Boland amendment, passed in October 1984. Administration critics were able to formally end congressional support for Contra aid in the wake of the mining episode and Representative Boland's own determination to maneuver his legislation through Congress. The House/Senate conference committee agreed upon language that prohibited the administration from funding the Contras. Before the final House vote, Boland said: "The compromise provision clearly ends U.S. support for the war in Nicaragua."[92] The relevant provision in the legislation appeared to be quite clear:

> No funds available to the Central Intelligence Agency, the Department of Defense, or any other agency or entity of the United States involved in intelligence activities may be obligated or expended for the purpose or which would have the effect of supporting, directly or indirectly, military or paramilitary operations in Nicaragua by any nation, group, organization, movement, or individual.[93]

After the passage of Boland II, Oliver North and the NSC staff assumed control of the Contras. For North and his network of supporters, Boland II could be circumvented by turning to other countries in their quest to find financial and military support for the Contra cause.[94]

Ronald Reagan had become increasingly strident in linking the Sandinistas to Cuba, the Soviet Union, and the spread of communism throughout the world. To Reagan, the Nicaraguan Contras, or "freedom fighters," were "the moral equivalent of the Founding Fathers."[95] Reagan had also been increasingly concerned about American hostages held hostage in Lebanon. It should be no surprise, then, that the administration continued to embrace covert actions as a viable way to bypass a hostile Congress and to promote American policy in Central America. Roy Gutman argues that Casey and North were merely carrying out Reagan's 1984 instruction to keep the Contras alive "body and soul" when Congress refused the CIA's request for additional Contra funding. Casey appealed to Reagan's romanticism as he continually reinforced Reagan's vision of the "freedom fighters," while North directed fund-raising and advised the rebels of political and military strategy.[96]

But who would have expected the Reagan administration to secretly sell arms to Iran's Ayatollah Khomeini in an effort to free American hostages? As a presidential candidate in 1980, Ronald Reagan had been particularly vitriolic in his criticism of Jimmy Carter's handling of the Iranian hostage situation and said that he would never negotiate with terrorists. Some have argued that it was actually William Casey who was the primary instigator of the arms-for-hostages swap.[97] But Reagan biographer Lou Cannon contends that such a perspective ignores Reagan's own central role in the Iran initiative: "It is too much to say that Casey preserved the Iran initiative. The prime mover of the initiative was Reagan himself, not North or Casey, and the president was determined to free the hostages by keeping the missiles flowing to Iran."[98]

Congressional hearings on the Iran-Contra affair revealed a number of disturbing aspects associated with the Reagan administration's conduct of foreign policy. First, there was very little accountability for covert operations in the Reagan era. In addition, the administration deceived Congress and the American people, revealed an unwillingness to subscribe to our system of checks and balances and the rule of law, and used private citizens to execute secret policy.[99] Finally, Reagan's own detached administrative style allowed North and Casey to formulate and implement the policies associated with the Iran-Contra affair. This created the permissive environment in which North and Casey pursued the policies that they had reason to believe would be supported by the president. Thus, they masterminded an incredible scheme where profits from the arms sales to Iran in exchange for hostages were diverted to the Contras. Under Casey, the CIA played a central role in these activities. The National Security Council, whose principal task was to "advise the President on all matters relating to national security,"[100] did little, save for circumventing the law by assisting in the organization and advising of a "private aid network to fund the contras,"[101] until President Reagan convened its members in the last days of the Iran-Contra crisis. Congress was also ignored by the Reagan White House.

If we accept Richard Falk's grim conclusion that "at no time in American history have the basic forms of popular democracy been so jeopardized, rendered vulnerable to dangerous and destructive forces,"[102] then the entire episode raises a number of disturbing questions. How could this happen in light of our recent experiences in the Vietnam War? Hadn't Congress passed legislation specifically designed to control the use of covert activities? Can Congress prevent presidents from engaging in such covert operations in the future? How might this goal be achieved? What would have been an appropriate congressional response to the transgressions committed by the Reagan White House? Is Congress even capable of responding in a meaningful way?

The Tower Commission report and the congressional Iran-Contra hearings failed to address these questions in the meaningful and effective way that a democratic society requires. Much attention was devoted to the Reagan administrative style without actually examining the content and consequences of his Central American and Middle Eastern policies. This is not to suggest that Congress is capable of addressing such issues satisfactorily. William Grover may well be right when he concludes that Congress is incapable of, and not interested in, restoring "balance to a foreign policy apparatus tilted toward the president." Perhaps Alexander Cockburn best captured the true spirit of the Iran-Contra congressional hearings: "True to gloomy predictions, Republicans, with the slack-jawed acquiescence and even vociferous support of most Democrats, have turned the joint congressional investigation into a pro-contra rally."[103]

One response to the Iran-Contra affair might have been to challenge the Reagan administration's adherence to a set of Cold War values that were at the foundation of American foreign policy in Central America. Another would be to press for impeachment of the president as well as prison terms for those involved in this sordid affair. Finally, the will and intent of Congress was ignored and thwarted in every conceivable way. But the most disturbing conclusion is that Congress failed to exercise its responsibilities as an equal partner in the conduct of American foreign policy. In this sense, Schlesinger's imperial presidency notion needs to be revised to take into account congressional acquiescence and judicial tolerance in foreign affairs. The post-Vietnam congressional reforms had little impact on presidential foreign policy power in the Reagan and Bush eras, nor did they challenge the ethnocentric notion that we have the right to maintain American hegemony throughout the world.[104] As Kenneth Sharpe has persuasively argued, if we are to challenge presidential aggrandizement of American foreign policy, then we must devise reforms that challenge the foreign policies growing out of our national security apparatus. This would also require confronting the Cold War assumptions underlying American foreign policy in the Reagan and Bush eras and our expectations of presidential achievement. Ultimately, it would mean challenging the dictates of the plebiscitary presidency.

The Plebiscitary Presidency and American Foreign Policy

The unilateral foreign policy actions discussed in this chapter have worked to institutionalize the plebiscitary presidency. As Barbara Hinckley has pointed out, "Presidents are expected to make foreign policy alone. Since constitutionally they cannot do so, they are forced to go outside the constitution to fulfill the expectations."[105] A central lesson of the Reagan and Bush eras is that presidents can solidify their popular support with attention to foreign policy concerns that promote American hegemony around the world and are rooted in patriotism. Because presidents recognize that they can bolster their public opinion stature and enhance their re-election chances, they may trigger international events merely to accomplish these goals.[106]

This is due to several factors. The conventional wisdom is that the public remains uninformed on foreign policy concerns, given the complexity of the issues involved and the fact that remote struggles around the world are of little interest.[107] Presidents, then, are given a virtual blank check to protect American interests unless, of course, the United States becomes involved in a protracted war such as Vietnam or a president and his close advisors engage in an unconstitutional act such as in the Iran-Contra affair.

The Reagan and Bush experiences suggest different strategies for enhancing presidential popularity. Richard Barnet concludes that "Ronald Reagan understood more clearly than any other politician of his time the symbolic importance of foreign policy in winning elections and in building presidential power." But what is interesting for our purposes is that Reagan largely disdained foreign policy during his first two years in office, apart from his consistent rhetorical attacks on the Soviet Union, his efforts to overthrow the Sandinistas, and his desire to promote the existing ruling regime in El Salvador. Reagan's primary concern was his domestic "revolution," in which he hoped to cut back federal government intervention by reducing taxes and regulations. It was his rhetorical foreign policy flourishes, however, that allowed Reagan to tap into powerful symbolism as he instilled in the American people that he was a leader who could tackle problems at home as well as fight the spread of communism throughout the world. The invasion of Grenada and the bombing of Libya provided concrete examples of a president who was willing to use military action to support his policy goals. His style of foreign policy leadership seemed to be particularly successful in the wake of the Iran hostage crisis and the prevailing sense that the Carter years were ones of weakness and vacillation in foreign affairs.[108] The Iran-Contra affair wounded Reagan severely, but he still left office as a very popular president (see Figure 3.1).

George Bush assumed office in 1989 after running a particularly empty and offensive campaign, one filled with domestic promises but very few details or a sustained commitment on how the so-called environmental and education president might achieve them. To no one's surprise, Bush soon gravitated toward his real interest—foreign policy. It soon became clear that he would much prefer to work with foreign leaders than congressional leaders. One persuasive explanation is that Bush recognizes the constitutional powers and consensual support he has in the foreign policy realm as opposed to the domestic policy arena where he must deal with a Democratically controlled Congress largely hostile to his domestic policy initiatives. Who can blame him for emphasizing foreign affairs, given the responses of Congress, the media, and the American people to the invasion of Panama and America's so-called victory in the Persian Gulf conflict? Bush's own public approval rating soared after each of these military engagements (see Figure 3.2). Some have suggested that Bush cannot count solely on his foreign policy successes if he wishes to insure his re-election in 1992.[109] Yet he was so popular in the afterglow of the Persian Gulf war that the Democrats had early trouble recruiting candidates to challenge him in the 1992 election.

Speaking to Congress in September 1990, President Bush offered his vision of "a new world order":

> Out of these troubled times a new world order can emerge from the threat of terror, stronger in the pursuit of justice and more secure in the quest for peace. An era in which the nations of the world, east and west, north and south, can prosper and live in harmony. A hundred generations have searched for this elusive path to peace, while a thousand wars raged across the span of human endeavor.[110]

Bush's own foreign policy style and actions in his first three years in office suggest that he views the executive as playing the central role in bringing his new world order vision to fruition. This view has been reinforced by the Congress, the American people, the media, and the Court. Yet it is inimical to democratic principles. If it is to be challenged, the American people must create an environment in which informed citizens can challenge the principles of the plebiscitary presidency and demand that Congress, as the institution most closely representative of the citizenry, play an equal role. This is not to suggest that Congress would necessarily arrive at different foreign policy decisions than the executive, for both operate within a set of values and principles committed to imparting America's resolve and interests around the world. Until this antiquated Cold War vision is challenged meaningfully at all levels of society, we can expect presidents to adhere to the plebiscitary presidency and continue to exercise the kind of presidential prerogative powers in foreign affairs that we have witnessed in the Reagan and Bush eras. How this vision might be challenged within the context of extending democracy and critical education for citizenship is the subject of the following chapter.

Notes

1. Quoted in Richard Rose, *The Postmodern President: George Bush Meets the World*, 2nd ed. (Chatham, New Jersey: Chatham House, 1991), p. 334.
2. See William F. Grover, *The President as Prisoner: A Structural Critique of the Carter and Reagan Years* (Albany: State University of New York Press, 1989), for an excellent statement of the structural approach as applied to presidential power.
3. William Pfaff, *Barbarian Sentiments: How the American Century Ends* (New York: Hill and Wang, 1989), p. 12.
4. Phil Williams, "The President and Foreign Relations," in Malcolm Shaw, ed., *The Modern Presidency: From Roosevelt to Reagan* (New York: Harper and Row, 1987), 1987, p. 206.
5. Pfaff, 1989, p. 9.
6. Helga Haftendorn, "Toward a Reconstruction of American Strength: A New Era in the Claim to Global Leadership?" in Haftendorn and Jakob Schissler, eds., *The Reagan Administration: A Reconstruction of American Strength?* (Berlin: Walter de Guyer, 1988), p. 3.
7. Jeff McMahan, *Reagan and the World: Imperial Policy in the New Cold War* (New York: Monthly Review Press, 1985), p. 11.
8. Pfaff, 1989, p. 13.
9. Thomas Cronin, *The State of the Presidency*, 2nd ed. (Boston: Little, Brown, 1980), p. 84.

10. Barbara Kellerman and Ryan J. Barilleaux, *The President as World Leader* (New York: St. Martin's Press, 1991), p. 37.

11. Edward S. Corwin, *The President: Office and Powers*, 4th ed. (New York: New York University Press, 1957), p. 171.

12. Theodore Draper, *A Very Thin Line: The Iran-Contra Affairs* (New York: Hill and Wang, 1991), pp. 582-583.

13. *Federalist #75*, p. 487.

14. Quoted in Draper, 1991, p. 583.

15. Harvey C. Mansfield, Jr., *Taming the Prince: The Ambivalence of Modern Executive Power* (New York: Free Press, 1989), p. 278.

16. Barbara Kellerman and Ryan Barilleaux, *The President as World Leader* (New York: St. Martin's, 1991), p. 41.

17. Quoted in David Gray Adler, "Presidential Prerogative and the National Security State: The Corruption of the Constitution." Paper prepared for the 1990 annual meeting of the American Political Science Association, San Francisco, California, August 30, 1990, pp. 15-16.

18. See Morris P. Fiorina, *Congress: The Keystone of the Washington Establishment*, 2nd ed. (New Haven: Yale University Press, 1989).

19. Kellerman and Barilleaux, 1991, p. 41.

20. Christopher Madison, "Bush's Breaks," *National Journal* March 10, 1990a, p. 564.

21. Randall B. Ripley, *Congress: Process and Policy*, 4th ed. (New York: Norton, 1988), p. 410.

22. Thomas E. Mann, "Making Foreign Policy: President and Congress," in Thomas E. Mann, ed., *A Question of Balance: The President, the Congress, and Foreign Policy* (Washington, D.C.: Brookings Institution, 1990), p. 1.

23. Madison, 1990a, p. 564.

24. Madison, 1990a, p. 566.

25. Kellerman and Barilleaux, 1991, p. 39.

26. Rose, 1991, p. 226.

27. Ripley, 1988, p. 415.

28. Christopher Madison, "No Blank Check," *National Journal* October 6, 1990, p. 2396.

29. Ryan J. Barilleaux, *The Post-Modern Presidency* (New York: Praeger Press, 1988), p. 10.

30. Mann, 1990, p. 20.

31. Daniel Paul Franklin, "War Powers in the Modern Context," *Congress and the Presidency* Spring 1987, Volume 14, Number 1, p. 82.

32. Franklin, 1987, p. 85.

33. Cecil V. Crabb, Jr., and Pat M. Holt, *Invitation to Struggle: Congress, the President, and Foreign Policy*, 3rd ed. (Washington, D.C.: Congressional Quarterly Press, 1989), p. 154.

34. Crabb and Holt, 1989, p. 145.

35. Jakob Schissler, "The Impact of the War Powers Resolution On Crisis Decisionmaking," in Helga Haftendorn and Jakob Schissler, eds. *The Reagan Administration: A Reconstruction of American Strength?* (Berlin: Walter de Guyer, 1988), pp. 223-224.

36. Crabb and Holt, 1989, p. 145.

37. Ronald Reagan quoted in Donald L. Robinson, *"To the Best of My Ability"*: *The Presidency and the Constitution* (New York: Norton, 1987), p. 253.

38. Robinson, 1987, p. 253.

39. Steven R. Weisman, "Reagan Signs Bill Allowing Marines to Stay in Beirut," *New York Times* October 13, 1983, p. A1.

40. Steven V. Roberts, "Legislators Say Reagan Must Reassess U.S. Role," *New York Times* October 24, 1983, p. A8.

41. Bernard Gwertzman, "Questions on Mission," *New York Times* October 24, 1983, p. A1.

42. Lou Cannon, *President Reagan: The Role of a Lifetime* (New York: Simon and Schuster, 1991), p. 390.

43. Schissler, 1988, p. 225.

44. Stuart Taylor, Jr., "Legality of Grenada Attack Disputed," *New York Times* October 26, 1983, p. A19.

45. Philip Taubman, "Senators Suggest Administration Exaggerated Its Cuba Assessment," *New York Times* October 30, 1983, p. A22.

46. See Bernard Gwertzman, "An Invasion Prompted by Previous Debacles," *New York Times* October 26, 1983, p. A1.

47. Steven V. Roberts, "Move in Congress," *New York Times* October 28, 1983, p. A1.

48. "Congress Reels Under Impact of Marine Deaths in Beirut, U.S. Invasion of Grenada," *Congressional Quarterly* October 29, 1983, Volume 41, p. 2215.

49. Taylor, 1983, p. A19.

50. Bernard Weinraub, "Qaddafi is Warned," *New York Times* April 16, 1986, p. A1.

51. Crabb and Holt, 1989, p. 150.

52. Crabb and Holt, 1989, pp. 150-151.

53. Crabb and Holt, 1989, p. 151.

54. John Felton, "In Wake of Libya, Skirmishing Over War Powers," *Congressional Quarterly* May 10, 1986, Volume 44, p. 1021.

55. Felton, 1986, p. 1022.

56. Linda Greenhouse, "Bill Would Give Reagan a Free Hand on Terror," *New York Times* April 18, 1986, p. A9.

57. See Bob Woodward, *The Commanders* (New York: Simon and Schuster, 1991), p. 85.

58. Woodward, 1991, p. 187.

59. See John Felton, "Bush, Hill Reach Agreement on Covert Action Issues," *Congressional Quarterly* October 28, 1989, Volume 47, p. 2884.

60. See Woodward, 1991, pp. 167-174, for a discussion of how President Bush and his trusted military officials reached the decision to invade.

61. See Pat Towell and John Felton, "Invasion, Noriega Ouster Win Support on Capitol Hill," *Congressional Quarterly* December 23, 1989, Volume 47, pp. 3532-3535.

62. Thomas L. Friedman, "Congress Generally Supports Attack, but Many Fear Consequences," *New York Times* December 21, 1989, p. A21.

63. Towell and Felton, 1989, p. 3535.

120   *The Plebiscitary Presidency*

64. See Martin Tolchin, "Legislators Express Concern on the Operation's Future," *New York Times* December 22, 1989, p. A20.

65. Richard E. Cohen, "Marching Through the War Powers Act," *National Journal* December 30, 1989, Volume 52, p. 3120.

66. Cohen, 1989, p. 3120.

67. All of these figures are taken from Woodward, 1991, p. 195.

68. Gavrielle Gemma and Teresa Gutierrez, "Introduction," *The U.S. Invasion of Panama: The Truth Behind Operation Just Cause.* Prepared by the Independent Commission of Inquiry on the U.S. Invasion of Panama (Boston: South End Press, 1991), p. 1.

69. See Noam Chomsky, *Deterring Democracy* (London: Verso, 1991), Chapter 5, for a discussion of Noriega's past relationship to the United States.

70. This list is taken from Larry Berman and Bruce W. Jentleson, "Bush and the Post-Cold War World: New Challenges for American Leadership," in Colin Campbell, S.J., and Bert A. Rockman, eds., *The Bush Presidency: First Appraisals* (Chatham, New Jersey: Chatham House, 1991), pp. 117-118.

71. Rose, 1991, p. 334.

72. Christopher Madison, "Sideline Players," *National Journal* December 15, 1990, Volume 50, p. 3024.

73. Madison, 1990, p. 3026.

74. Christopher Madison, "Will Bush Ask for an OK Before War?" *National Journal* November 10, 1990b, p. 2751.

75. See Woodward, 1991, for a discussion of Bush's decision to go to war and the advice he received from Baker and Powell.

76. Joan Biskupic, "Constitutional Questions Remain," *Congressional Quarterly* January 12, 1991, Volume 49, p. 70.

77. See Woodward, 1991, pp. 356-357.

78. Berman and Jentleson, 1991, p. 117.

79. Berman and Jentleson, 1991, p. 122.

80. Benjamin Ginsberg and Martin Shefter, "After the Reagan Revolution: A Postelectoral Politics," in Larry Berman, ed., *Looking Back on the Reagan Presidency* (Baltimore: Johns Hopkins University Press, 1990), p. 248.

81. Crabb and Holt, 1989, p. 174.

82. Cynthia J. Arnson, *Crossroads: Congress, the Reagan Administration, and Central America* (New York: Pantheon, 1989), pp. 14-15.

83. Draper, 1991, p. 14.

84. Draper, 1991, p. 14.

85. Draper, 1991, p. 14.

86. Harold Hongju Koh, "Why the President (Almost) Always Wins in Foreign Affairs: Lessons of the Iran-Contra Affair," *The Yale Law Journal* June 1988, Volume 97, Number 7, p. 1258.

87. Roy Gutman, *Banana Diplomacy: The Making of American Policy in Nicaragua, 1981-1987* (New York: Simon and Schuster, 1988), p. 36.

88. Crabb and Holt, 1989, p. 183.

89. Crabb and Holt, 1989, p. 184.

90. Draper, 1991, p. 20.

91. Draper, 1991, p. 23.

92. Arnson, 1989, p. 167.

93. Arnson, 1989, pp. 167-168.

94. Draper, 1991, p. 93.

95. *Weekly Compilation of Presidential Documents* (Washington, D.C.: Office of the Federal Register, National Archives and Records Service, General Services Administration), March 11, 1985, p. 245.

96. Gutman, 1988, p. 313.

97. See, for example, Bob Woodward, *Veil: The Secret Wars of the CIA, 1981-1987* (New York: Simon and Schuster, 1987).

98. Cannon, 1991, p. 637.

99. Larry Berman, ed., *Looking Back on the Reagan Presidency* (Baltimore: Johns Hopkins University Press, 1990), p. 13.

100. Draper, 1991, p. 4.

101. Kenneth E. Sharpe, "The Post-Vietnam Formula under Siege: The Imperial Presidency and Central America," *Political Science Quarterly* Winter 1987-1988, Volume 102, Number 4, p. 562.

102. Richard Falk, "Preface," in Jonathan Marshall, Peter Dale Scott, and Jane Hunter, *The Iran-Contra Connection* (Boston: South End Press, 1987) p. xi.

103. Grover, 1989, pp. 172-173.

104. See Sharpe, 1987-1988, for an excellent discussion of these issues.

105. Barbara Hinckley, *The Symbolic Presidency: How Presidents Portray Themselves* (New York: Routledge, Chapman and Hall, 1990), p. 145.

106. See Theodore J. Lowi, in Michael Nelson, ed., "An Aligning Election: A Presidential Plebiscite," *The Elections of 1984* (Washington, D.C.: Congressional Quarterly Press, 1985), p. 295.

107. Richard J. Barnet, *The Rockets' Red Glare: When America Goes to War* (New York: Simon and Schuster, 1990), p. 18.

108. Barnet, 1990, pp. 369-370.

109. See, for example, John Dillin, "Public Wants Bush to Shift Focus to Domestic Issues, Pollsters Say," *Christian Science Monitor* July 25, 1991, p. 1.

110. Rose, 1991, p. 336.

6

Hero Worship and the Decline of Citizenship

Only the Constitution overshadows the Presidency as an object of popular reverence, and the Constitution does not walk about smiling and waving.
—Clinton Rossiter, *The American Presidency*

This book has shown that if presidents wish to meet the heightened citizen expectations associated with the plebiscitary presidency, they will turn to power sources that have been institutionalized in the modern era. The constitutional framers assured this situation when they failed to clearly conceptualize presidential powers and responsibilities. Presidents have come to rely on public opinion support and their own ability to exercise executive prerogative in the face of a vaguely rendered constitutional statement of presidential authority in domestic and foreign affairs. It is ironic that as the framers attempted to curtail presidential power by creating a system of separate institutions sharing (in some cases) vaguely defined powers, they actually guaranteed that presidents in the twentieth century would turn to alternative sources of presidential prerogative power to meet the heightened citizen expectations of the modern era.

As we have seen, these presidential power sources have manifested themselves in a number of ways. For example, the Reagan administration did particularly well in using the rhetorical presidency to provide the appearance of presidential accomplishments. The rise of the rhetorical presidency affords presidents new opportunities to influence the congressional policymaking process in the absence of the coherent political parties needed to build the necessary coalitions for effective governance. The rhetorical presidency becomes important as presidents attempt to build the public opinion support that is needed to successfully work with Congress and the rest of the executive branch, as well as to guide American foreign policy.

Presidents can now turn to an administrative strategy characterized by the use of various prerogative powers and a partisan approach to the presidential appointment process. Both the Reagan and Bush presidencies were successful in using the institutionalized presidency to expand presidential powers and to codify conservative ideological principles into concrete public policy.

The Reagan and Bush experiences also suggest that presidents should use a values strategy as a central component in their electoral campaigns and as a strategy for governance. Such a strategy is effective if presidents articulate clearly and convincingly the classical liberal values of individualism and freedom, equality of opportunity, hard work, religiosity, and free enterprise values that underlie American exceptionalism. Yet a value strategy is not enough; if presidents wish to achieve policy success, they must move beyond the rhetorical powers of the office and devote renewed attention to their legislative and administrative strategies. This has surely been the lesson of George Bush's first term as he struggles to achieve even a modicum of success in domestic policy.

The Reagan and Bush experiences in foreign policy suggest that through the years, presidents have assumed—at the expense of Congress and the citizenry—considerable foreign policymaking powers that threaten democratic accountability and the principles of representative government. Presidents can enjoy a considerable amount of popularity by addressing foreign policy concerns that reinforce American interests and values throughout the world. George Bush, in particular, has found that pursuing foreign policy concerns can help to meet the heightened citizen expectations associated with the plebiscitary presidency. This is particularly true for a president who has revealed little interest in domestic policy. Presidents Reagan and Bush have found ways to exercise executive foreign policy prerogative in the face of Congress's ill-defined role and its unwillingness to seek out more opportunities for a meaningful role in foreign affairs. Presidents who wish to enjoy at least short-term popularity will turn to foreign policy opportunities as a way to bolster American values throughout the world, divert the public's attention from domestic ills (especially in times of limited fiscal resources), and reinforce their symbolic position as the nation's central figure.

The president's symbolic role and its consequences for the plebiscitary presidency and reform of the American political system are the subjects to which we now turn. This chapter also includes a discussion of how we might develop a pedagogical strategy and evaluation scheme that can challenge the central elements of the plebiscitary presidency.

Symbolic Politics and Presidential Power

In the American political system, presidents perform two roles that in other countries are often filled by separate individuals. As head of the nation, the president is required to play a unifying role of the kind played by monarchs in Britain, Norway, and the Netherlands or by presidents in France, Germany, and Austria. In addition, presidents serve as political leaders, "a post held in these other nations by a prime minister or chancellor."[1] This dual role virtually guarantees that American presidents will occupy the central political and cultural role as the chief spokesperson for the American way of life. Political scientists, historians, and journalists have all reinforced and popularized the view that the presidency is an office of overwhelming symbolic importance.

Only recently have political scientists begun to challenge this perspective and discuss the negative consequences of such hero worship in a country that purports to adhere to democratic principles. Barbara Hinckley captures these issues well in her recent analysis:

> It is the magic of symbolism to create illusion. But illusion has costs that must be considered by journalists, teachers of politics, and future presidents. Is the nation best served by carrying on the symbolism or by challenging it? Should the two contradictory pictures, in a kind of schizophrenic fashion, be carried on together? If so, what line should be drawn and what accommodation made between the two? The questions are compounded by the peculiar openness of the office to changing interpretations. By definition, all institutions are shaped by the expectations of relevant actors. The presidency is particularly susceptible to such influence.[2]

As we have seen in our study of the Reagan and Bush presidencies, presidents attempt to build on their symbolic importance to enhance their public opinion ratings and to extend the plebiscitary presidency. The upshot of this activity over the past sixty years is that the public equates the president with the nation and the values associated with American exceptionalism. A president, such as Jimmy Carter, who attempts to challenge traditional elements of presidential symbolism and demystify the trappings of the White House, is treated with disdain by the public, the press, and to a certain extent by political scientists.

The principles of democratic governance are better served if we challenge the lofty expectations of presidential performance and the concomitant attention that presidents devote to reinforcing the symbolic aspects of their office rather than concentrating their attention on innovative and substantive policy proposals. This requires that we move beyond the institutional and procedural reforms that have been offered in recent years to address a divided government and "the deadlock of democracy." In order to challenge the existing concept of the presidency, we must extend Hinckley's analysis by examining the connection between leadership and followership and the consequences of that connection for democratic theory and practice.

A first step may be to challenge the kind of transforming leadership that is often accepted blindly by political scientists and reinforced by presidents who attempt to meet the dictates of the plebiscitary presidency. James MacGregor Burns contends that "the transforming leader recognizes and exploits an existing need or demand of a potential follower. But beyond that, the transforming leader looks for potential motives in followers, seeks to satisfy higher needs, and engages the full person of the follower."[3] Burns's analysis leaves us with several important questions that grow out of the issues raised in this book: Why do citizens look to the presidency for transforming leadership? What is the source of such dependency? Can any president ever meet such high expectations of presidential performance? To what extent can such a vision of leadership be squared with democratic principles? What reforms, if any, can be offered to fundamentally challenge such a leadership vision? This chapter will attempt to address these questions.

Evaluating Presidential Performance

A presidential evaluation scheme and pedagogical strategy must take into account institutional constraints and must recognize the importance of adhering to principles of democratic accountability as presidents wrestle with difficult redistributive issues. Bruce Buchanan has asked: "What criteria for choosing presidents and judging their performance can yield adequate levels of public support, while simultaneously holding presidents to account for their effectiveness in office?"[4] He argues persuasively that if political scientists do not link an evaluation of presidential performance to democratic accountability and citizenship, this failure "could ultimately result in a diminution of citizen power."

Recent events in Eastern Europe, the Soviet Union, and China afford American political scientists the opportunity to critically confront their own democratic form. By linking democratic theory, democratic practice, and issues of pedagogy, political scientists can begin to tackle questions of leadership and followership in challenging the fundamental assumptions of the plebiscitary presidency. In this discussion these questions are addressed within the context of a capitalist political economy rooted in the politics of privatism and coexisting with the republican form.

Meaningful and Effective Participation

The problem of defining meaningful and effective citizen participation pervades much of the participatory democracy literature. But a thorough examination of participatory democratic arguments reveals that three elements must be present if meaningful and effective citizen participation is to be achieved: (1) a sense of community identity; (2) education and the development of citizenship; and (3) self-determination by those participating.[5]

Proponents of participatory democracy argue that increased citizen participation in community and workplace decisionmaking is important if people are to recognize their roles and responsibilities as citizens within the larger community. Community meetings, for example, afford citizens knowledge regarding other citizens' needs. In a true participatory setting, citizens do not merely act as autonomous individuals pursuing their own interests, but instead through a process of decision, debate, and compromise, they ultimately link their concerns with the needs of the community.

The arguments for participatory democracy are based on two additional tenets: (1) a belief that increased citizen participation will contribute both to the development of the individual and to the individual's realization of citizenship; and (2) a belief that individuals should participate in community and workplace decisions that will affect the quality and direction of their lives. Each of these tenets is grounded in a positive conception of liberty.[6]

Proponents of participatory democracy extend the Rousseauean notion that citizen participation in decisionmaking has a favorable psychological effect on those participating. Carole Pateman argues that through participation in political decisionmaking, the individual learns to be a public as well as a private citizen.[7]

Besides developing the individual's creative capacities, participation in decisionmaking encourages the individual to become more informed regarding the political process. Citizen participation theorists such as Benjamin Barber emphasize the beneficial learning process that is afforded to all those who participate with and talk to one another in community decisionmaking.[8] From this perspective, the political education, rather than socialization, of the individual will be practiced wherever increased citizen participation is encouraged.

A third component of the participatory democratic model is based on the notion that individuals from all classes in society must share in those decisions determining the quality and direction of their lives. From this vantage point, important community decisions should not be made solely by bureaucrats and elected officials. If the multiple perspectives of those involved are to be consulted, the group decision process is essential. Individuals who participate in the local decision-making process will be afforded a sense of participation and commitment that is otherwise nonexistent in a system where elites rule the policymaking and implementation process. Besides permitting individuals to realize self-development and practice citizenship, participatory democracy ideally wrests the policy implementation process away from the elite and allows citizens to have a say in those decisions affecting their lives. In so doing, it challenges the fundamental assumptions of leadership and followership associated with the plebiscitary presidency.

The Revisionist Critique

What the traditional participatory democratic model lacks, however, is an awareness of the particular barriers faced by women and minorities as they attempt to achieve full citizenship. In recent years, groups who have been relegated to the margins of American society have drawn increased attention to the important issue of standpoint and its relationship to power.

Feminist studies of women's political participation offer an alternative discourse on citizenship, as Kathleen Jones suggests in a recent review essay that examines much of this important literature.[9] Essays by Lisa Disch and Leslie Hill do well in articulating a number of important arguments regarding a feminist conception of citizenship. Disch is surely on target when she argues that a major contribution of feminist critical theory is how it "shifts the study of gender from individuals' roles and identities to the study of the interplay between gender relations and the institutional contexts within which they take place."[10] Leslie Hill broadens the discussion considerably by concluding that "examining participation in public life at the margins is a critical step in highlighting alternative approaches to power relations and citizenship practice especially for students and others who feel alienated from contemporary politics."[11] By making the crucial connection among gender, race, and class, Hill offers political science teachers the means of linking power and participation with the outcomes of the public policy process.

Hill's work also provides a number of practical suggestions for scholars and teachers wrestling with issues of democratic theory and leadership. The civil rights and women's movements are examples of "free spaces,"[12] where communitarian values and goals are prevalent. The relationship of leadership and followership in these two movements deserves serious and sustained attention by those who want to challenge the dictates of the plebiscitary presidency.

Critical Education for Citizenship

Habermas's notion of the "open public sphere" is a useful pedagogical construct for examining the possibilities of achieving a participatory democracy in the United States.[13] This notion has already been used quite successfully to evaluate democratic movements in other countries, such as the Polish solidarity movement.[14] Habermas identifies three elements of the open public sphere: publicity and openness; undistorted communication among citizens; and a society that is not state or market centered. The United States does not really come close to approximating Habermas's vision. A course devoted to questions of leadership and democratic theory should evaluate whether the "open public sphere" is desirable, how feminist and minority critiques might make Habermas's conception of participation more accessible to all classes and groups in society, and in what arenas such participation is achievable. The question of why the United States falls so short of this vision must also be addressed.

One answer to that question is that the constitutional framers created a number of structural barriers designed to reduce and restrain the power and participation of the citizenry in order to achieve systemic stability in both the short and long term. These barriers include stringent property qualifications designed to limit uninformed and passionate citizen participation in public affairs, indirect elections of senators, and the creation of the Electoral College for electing the president. The underlying rationale for the framers' efforts can be gleaned from a thorough examination of *The Federalist*. Considerable attention might also be devoted to examining the republican form with the ultimate goal of evaluating "the tensions between republicanism, with its strong historical attraction to elitism, and democracy."[15]

A second reason that the United States falls short of the participatory democratic vision is rooted in the inequalities in the distribution of property, wealth, and resources that have been imbedded in the American political economy since its conception. These inequalities have yet to be addressed by our limited American welfare state. For citizens who must continually struggle to obtain quality health care, education, decent housing, and a stable job, it will be difficult to find the time and commitment needed to participate in the ways that Habermas describes. Instead, they typically turn to political leaders, most notably the president, to insure that their basic economic needs are met. Presidents recognize that this element of the plebiscitary presidency will be increasingly difficult to meet in a time of increased austerity. It is this "expectations gap"[16] that will continue to fuel citizen unhappiness with presidential performance, as both Ronald Reagan and George Bush have learned.

The political socialization process also impedes meaningful and effective participation because citizens are socialized to embrace the values of privatism and radical individualism that emanate from capitalism. For a true communitarian vision to prevail, such a socialization process would have to be challenged and transformed. Despite the fact that the United States calls itself a democracy, it lacks a strong democratic culture. As Richard Flacks has pointed out, Americans are socialized to accept political inactivity and the notion that history should be determined by elites rather than the larger citizenry. Citizenship in America is identified with merely voting in periodic elections,[17] and public opinion polls are used to measure citizen satisfaction with presidential performance. Such polls thus become a central element of the plebiscitary presidency and reinforce notions of followership and passivity on the part of the citizenry.[18]

Demystifying the Modern Presidency

Any course on the modern American presidency surely must challenge James MacGregor Burns's claim that "leaders help transform followers' needs into positive hopes and aspirations."[19] Burns' notion of leadership reinforces the central assumptions of the plebiscitary presidency. What it fails to recognize is the structural, institutional, and cultural constraints facing any president. A central theme of presidency literature during the 1980s and early 1990s is the need to recognize institutional limits on presidents' abilities to translate their campaign promises into concrete public policy.[20] Scholars have argued that the so-called "text-book presidency"[21] paints an unrealistic picture of presidential power within the confines of a Madisonian framework of separate institutions sharing power. Others have accurately said that this unrealistic vision has contributed to the "cult of the presidency,"[22] which is reinforced by the political socialization process and the media, thus leading to the "no-win"[23] or "impossible"[24] presidencies. The notion of a plural executive, whose powers are fragmented throughout the Madisonian system, has also grown in popularity.[25] As a part of their recommendations for reform, virtually all presidential scholars emphasize the role of educators in imparting a more realistic understanding of the limits on presidential power and outlining the potential consequences of hero worship for the occupant of the Oval Office. If political scientists wish to challenge the plebiscitary presidency notion, then they must embrace an approach to teaching about the presidency that rejects the notion that the president should be the most important actor in the American political system. Instead, students must be asked to consider the president as one actor in a highly fragmented political system and to develop a more realistic view of both the sources and uses of presidential power within the broader context of leadership, democratic accountability, and the development of critical education for citizenship.

Political Socialization and the American Presidency

If students are to understand the sources of their own expectations of presidential performance, they should study the political socialization process. As discussed in Chapter 3, studies of political socialization and the American presidency reveal that the contemporary president is expected to be strong, assertive, virtuous, and, above all, a savior.[26] Bruce Buchanan concludes that the American people perceive that the "presidency has the potential to make extraordinary events happen, and as the institution's central figure, the incumbent president should be able to realize that potential."[27] Students need opportunities to discuss their own expectations of presidential performance and what constitutes exemplary presidential leadership and reflect upon the sources of these beliefs. The consequences of heightened expectations for presidential performance and the forces ultimately perpetuating unrealistic images are also intriguing discussion topics.

The importance of the presidency as a potent political symbol should also be considered. Theodore Lowi is surely on target when he identifies "the refocusing of mass expectations upon the presidency" as a key problem of presidential governance since FDR and a problem associated with the rise of the plebiscitary presidency.[28] The constitutional framers would hardly have approved of this development, for they had no intention of establishing "a monarch of any kind."[29] While students may revere the American Constitution, many have little understanding of its underlying principles or the nature of the lengthy Constitutional Convention debates over separation of powers, checks and balances, and the office of the executive. Presidency courses should devote sustained attention to the framers' intentions and the consequences of their decisions for the role of the presidency in the American domestic and foreign policy processes today.

The Presidency in a Time of Resource Scarcity

If students are to challenge the prevailing textbook view of the primacy of the presidency in the American political system, they should consider whether presidents will be able to meet the heightened expectations of presidential performance associated with the plebiscitary presidency. Students should be asked to conceptualize presidential decisionmaking in an environment of increased resource scarcity. Resource scarcity refers to the possibility that future generations will endure a standard of living below our own as energy resources become more scarce.[30] At a more narrow but related level, resource scarcity refers to shrinking budgets for various governmental programs as policymakers attempt to meet the concerns of citizens and their demands on presidential performance. Will the framers' system of separation of powers and checks and balances allow political actors to meet the concerns of all classes in society during a time of increased resource scarcity? This is a compelling question that has generated considerable scholarly discussion[31] and has important implications for the plebiscitary presidency. It also is worthy of attention in a course on the presidency.

Presidential Coalition Building and Party Decline

Linking the presidential selection process to strategies for governance is one teaching approach to challenging the "textbook presidency." An intensive discussion of the role of political parties in the electoral and governing processes is essential if students are to fully understand the development of the presidency in the modern era. Analysts have argued that "the decline in the role of parties as the linkage between a president's electoral support and governing support has made it more difficult for presidents to build stable governing coalitions, thus making presidential influence more variable and unstable."[32] As a result, presidents must now build their own coalitions once they assume office. As Chapter 3 points out, the absence of the coherent political parties needed to build effective governing coalitions has forced presidents to rely increasingly upon media manipulation and "going public" to go over the heads of Congress and appeal for support from the American people directly.[33] President Bush has been especially constrained by his reluctance to raise taxes and by the massive budget deficit left by his predecessor. How presidents deal with a political environment marked by fiscal austerity is a compelling feature of what Barilleaux identifies as the postmodern presidency.[34] A discussion of the president's and

Congress's roles in the budgetary process, in light of the Congressional Budget and Impoundment Control Act of 1974 and the 1986 Gramm-Rudman-Hollings legislation, offers students an opportunity to reflect upon the constraints confronting President Bush and his successors. The increasing fragmentation of the executive branch and the inability of the president to control the vast bureaucracy through cabinet appointments asks students to confront the failure of presidents to meet the demands of the textbook presidency. A discussion of the administrative strategies used by past presidents, especially Nixon and Reagan,[36] provides an excellent vehicle for detailing how past presidents have dealt with these constraints.

The Plebiscitary Presidency and Foreign Policy

This book suggests that Presidents Reagan and Bush turned to foreign policy when they encountered difficulties in translating their domestic campaign promises into concrete public policy and in meeting the demands of the plebiscitary presidency. Presidents who are caught between citizens' expectations and the constraints of the Madisonian policymaking process look to the foreign policy arena in an effort to promote the values associated with American exceptionalism.

Any of the examples discussed in Chapter 5 provide ample opportunity to explore these themes. The Iran-Contra affair, in particular, raises compelling questions regarding presidential power in the foreign policy arena. In light of the aggrandizement of presidential power that characterized the Vietnam War period and Watergate and the resulting congressional response, it is important to ask students why a president and/or his staff would employ some of the same strategies in dealing with Congress, the media, and the American people. The role of covert activities in a democracy also deserves considerable attention.

If scholars of the presidency are truly concerned with developing a pedagogy and presidential evaluation scheme rooted in critical education for citizenship, then their students must be asked to consider why so little questioning generally occurs regarding the role of the president in committing American troops to war. The Persian Gulf war was a case in point. It begged for serious discussion, reflection, debate, and questioning about the Bush administration's foreign policy decision-making. Some argued that those who dissented from the president's foreign policy strategy were un-American and unpatriotic and were trying to undermine the troops who were already in the Middle East. In fact, if citizens fail to question a president's decisionmaking, then they are giving the president virtually unchecked power to do what he wants with their lives. The failure to question a president abdicates all of the principles of a meaningful and effective democracy and embraces the dictates of an authoritarian and totalitarian regime. This is, of course, the logical consequence of the plebiscitary presidency.

Alexis de Tocqueville spoke of a blind and unreflective patriotism that characterized the American citizenry during the nineteenth century. He would surely see evidence of such patriotism in America today. There is little doubt that such patriotism can be connected to the relationship of the citizenry to the state and the office of the presidency. No modern president can expect to succeed without the support of the public. Yet this support must be grounded in a firm rejection of the unrealistic notion of presidential power. Citizens who respond to the presidency in a highly personalized and reverential manner are likely to be disappointed by presidential performance and are also likely to embrace political passivity and acquiescence in the face of presidential power. In the words of Benjamin Barber, "democratic politics thus becomes a matter of what leaders do, something that citizens watch rather than something they do."[36] As this book has pointed out, Ronald Reagan and George Bush heightened these expectations even further by using techniques that emphasize the plebiscitary, personal character of the modern presidency. Ross Perot's 1992 presidential campaign was firmly rooted in plebiscitary principles. His proposals for nation-wide town meetings and an electronic democracy scheme reflected support for government by plebiscite. To Perot, running as an outsider, anti-establishment candidate, such a plan was desperately needed to challenge the gridlock growing out of the Madisonian policy process and two party system. His proposals also enabled him to emphasize his own leadership abilities and claim that he had the necessary leadership and entrepreneurial abilities to break governmental paralysis. In doing so, Perot reinforced the direct line between the presidency and the American people. Any course on the presidency should examine Perot's government-by-plebiscite proposals and the broader implications of his apparent willingness to bypass the congressional policy process and the two party system. The amount of attention and popularity that Perot's campaign garnered in a short period of time suggests once again that the plebiscitary presidency is an important explanatory construct. It also encourages political scientists to study, with renewed vigor, the relationship between the presidency and the citizenry.

For many students, the presidency is the personification of democratic politics and, as a result, monopolizes "the public space."[37] This view impedes the development of the meaningful and effective participation needed by citizens as they attempt to control decisions that affect the quality and direction of their lives. Presidential scholars have developing a more realistic understanding of the changing sources of presidential power and how individual presidents have used these powers through the years. We would also do well to consider Murray Edelman's claim that "leadership is an expression of the inadequate power of followers in their everyday lives."[38] This is particularly important as we begin to evaluate the Bush presidency. It is also the first step toward challenging the plebiscitary presidency and achieving a more realistic and successful presidency, one that is grounded in principles of democratic accountability and the development of citizenship.

Notes

1. Joseph A. Pika, "Reaching Out to Organized Interests: Public Liaison in the Modern White House," in Richard Waterman, ed., *The Presidency Reconsidered* (Itasca, Illinois: Peacock Press, forthcoming), p. 2.

2. Barbara Hinckley, *The Symbolic Presidency: How Presidents Portray Themselves* (New York: Routledge, Chapman and Hall, 1990), p. 138.

3. James MacGregor Burns, *Leadership* (New York: Harper and Row, 1978), p. 4.

4. Bruce Buchanan, *The Citizen's Presidency* (Washington, D.C.: Congressional Quarterly Press, 1987), p. 3.

5. See Carole Pateman, *Participation and Democratic Theory* (Cambridge: Cambridge University Press, 1970); C.B. Macpherson, *The Life and Times of Liberal Democracy* (Oxford: Oxford University Press, 1976); and Ronald M. Mason, *Participatory and Workplace Democracy: A Theoretical Development in the Critique of Liberalism* (Carbondale: Southern Illinois University Press, 1982).

6. See Isaiah Berlin, *Four Essays on Liberty* (Oxford: Oxford University Press, 1969).

7. Pateman, 1970.

8. See Benjamin R. Barber, *Strong Democracy: Participatory Politics for a New Age* (Berkeley: University of California Press, 1984).

9. See Kathleen B. Jones, "Citizenship in a Woman-Friendly Polity" (Review Essay), *Signs: Journal of Women in Culture and Society*, 1990, Volume 15, Number 4.

10. See Lisa M. Disch, "Toward a Feminist Conception of Politics," *PS: Political Science and Politics* September 1991, Volume 24, pp. 501-504.

11. See Leslie I. Hill, "Power and Citizenship in a Democratic Society," *PS: Political Science and Politics* September 1991, Volume 24, pp. 495-498.

12. See Sara M. Evans and Harry C. Boyte, *Free Spaces: The Sources of Democratic Change in America* (New York: Harper and Row, 1986), for a discussion of "free spaces."

13. Jurgen Habermas, *The Structural Transformation of the Public Sphere* (Cambridge: Cambridge University Press, 1989).

14. See David Ost, *Solidarity and the Politics of Anti-Politics: Opposition and Reform in Poland Since 1968* (Philadelphia: Temple University Press, 1989).

15. Sheldon Wolin, "Introduction," in Wolin, ed., *The Presence of the Past: Essays on the State and the Constitution* (Baltimore: Johns Hopkins University Press, 1989), p. 5.

16. See Richard W. Waterman, ed., *The Presidency Reconsidered* (Itasca, Illinois: Peacock Press, forthcoming).

17. See Richard Flacks, *Making History* (New York: Columbia University Press, 1988).

18. For a discussion of how public opinion surveys actually undermine democratic principles, see John S. Dryzek, "The Mismeasure of Political Man," *The Journal of Politics* 1988, Number 50, pp. 705-725.

19. Burns, 1978, p. 117.

20. See, for example, Harold M. Barger, *The Impossible Presidency:Illusions and Realities of Presidential Power* (Glenview, Illinois: Scott Foresman, 1984); Thomas E. Cronin, *The State of the Presidency*, 2nd ed., (Boston: Little, Brown, 1980); Barbara Hinckley, *Problems of the Presidency: A Text with Readings* (Chicago: Scott, Foresman, 1985); and Paul C. Light, *The President's Agenda: With Notes on Ronald Reagan* (Baltimore: Johns Hopkins University Press, 1983).

21. See Cronin, 1980.

22. Hinckley, 1985.

23. Light, 1983.

24. Barger, 1984.

25. Gary W. King and Lyn Ragsdale, *The Elusive Executive: Discovering Statistical Patterns in the Presidency* (Washington, D.C.: Congressional Quarterly Press, 1988).

26. Steven J. Wayne, *The Road to the White House*, 2nd ed. (New York: St. Martin's Press, 1984).

27. Buchanan, 1987, p. 28.

28. Theodore J. Lowi, *The Personal President: Power Invested and Promise Unfulfilled* (Ithaca: Cornell University Press, 1985), p. 100.

29. Hugh Brogan, *The Longman History of the United States of America* (New York: William Morrow, 1985), p. 216.

30. See Richard J. Barnet, *The Lean Years: Politics in the Age of Scarcity* (New York: Touchstone, 1980); Paul Blumberg, *Inequality in an Age of Decline* (Oxford: Oxford University Press, 1980); Robert L. Heilbroner, *An Inquiry into the Human Prospect: Looked at Again for the 1990's* (New York: Norton, 1991); William Ophuls, *Ecology and the Politics of Scarcity* (San Francisco: W.H. Freeman, 1977).

31. See, for example, James MacGregor Burns, *The Power to Lead: The Crisis of the American Presidency* (New York: Simon and Schuster, 1984), and James L. Sundquist, *Constitutional Reform and Effective Government* (Washington, D.C.: Brookings Institution, 1986).

32. Lester G. Seligman and Cary R. Covington, *The Coalitional Presidency* (Chicago: Richard Irwin, 1989), p. 2.

33. See Hedrick Smith, *The Power Game* (New York: Simon and Schuster, 1988).

34. See Ryan J. Barilleaux, *The Post-Modern Presidency* (New York: Praeger, 1988).

35. See Richard Nathan, *The Administrative Presidency* (New York: John Wiley and Sons, 1983), for an excellent discussion of Nixon's and Reagan's uses of the administrative strategy.

36. Benjamin Barber, "Neither Leaders Nor Followers: Citizenship Under Strong Democracy," in Michael R. Beschloss and Thomas E. Cronin, eds., *Essays in Honor of James MacGregor Burns* (Englewood Cliffs, New Jersey: Prentice-Hall, 1989), p. 121.

37. See Bruce Miroff, "Monopolizing the Public Space: The President as a Problem for Democratic Politics," in Thomas Cronin, ed., *Rethinking the Presidency* (Boston: Little, Brown, 1982), for a discussion of how the president monopolizes "the public space."

38. Murray Edelman, *Constructing the Political Spectacle* (Chicago: University of Chicago Press, 1988), p. 62.

Bibliography

Abramson, Jeffrey B., F. Christopher Arterton, and Gary R. Orren. *The Electronic Commonwealth: The Impact of New Media Technologies on Democratic Politics*. New York: Basic Books, 1988.

Adler, David Gray. "Presidential Prerogative and the National Security State: The Corruption of the Constitution." Paper prepared for delivery at the 1990 Annual Meeting of the American Political Science Association, San Francisco, California, August 30, 1990.

Aldrich, John H., and Thomas Weko. "The Presidency and the Election Process: Campaign Strategy, Voting, and Governance," in *The Elections of 1984*, ed. Michael Nelson. Washington, D.C.: Congressional Quarterly Press, 1985.

Anderson, Martin. *Revolution*. New York: Harcourt Brace Jovanovich, 1988.

Apple, R. W. "Sununu Tells How and Why He Pushed Souter for Court." *New York Times*, July 25, 1990, p. A-12.

Arnold, Peri E. *Making the Managerial Presidency*. Princeton, New Jersey: Princeton University Press, 1986.

Arnson, Cynthia J. *Crossroads: Congress, the Reagan Administration, and Central America*. New York: Pantheon, 1989.

Barber, Benjamin. "Neither Leaders Nor Followers: Citizenship Under Strong Democracy," in *Essays in Honor of James MacGregor Burns*, eds. Michael R. Beschloss and Thomas E. Cronin. Englewood Cliffs, New Jersey: Prentice-Hall, 1989.

_____. "The Compromised Republic: Public Purposelessness in America," in *The Moral Foundations of the American Republic*, 3rd ed., ed. Richard Hofstader. Charlottesville: University of Virginia Press, 1986.

_____. *Strong Democracy: Participatory Politics for a New Age*. Berkeley: University of California Press, 1984.

Barger, Harold M. *The Impossible Presidency: Illusions and Realities of Presidential Power*. Glenview, Illinois: Scott Foresman, 1984.

Barilleaux, Ryan J. *The Post-Modern Presidency*. New York: Praeger, 1988.

Barnes, James A. "Out on his Own." *National Journal* 23 (June 6, 1987): 1452-1456.

Barnet, Richard J. *The Rockets' Red Glare: When America Goes to War.* New York: Simon and Schuster, 1990.

———. *The Lean Years: Politics in the Age of Scarcity.* New York: Touchstone, 1980.

Bellah, Robert N., Richard Madsen, William M. Sullivan, Ann Swidler, and Steven M. Tipton. *Habits of the Heart: Individualism and Commitment in American Life.* New York: Harper and Row, 1985.

Benda, Peter M., and Charles H. Levine. "Reagan and the Bureaucracy: The Bequest, the Promise, and the Legacy," in *The Reagan Legacy: Promise and Performance*, ed. Charles O. Jones. Chatham, New Jersey: Chatham House, 1988.

Berlin, Isaiah. *Four Essays on Liberty.* Oxford: Oxford University Press, 1969.

Berman, Larry, ed. *Looking Back on the Reagan Presidency.* Baltimore: Johns Hopkins University Press, 1990.

Berman, Larry, and Bruce W. Jentleson. "Bush and the Post-Cold War World: New Challenges for American Leadership," in *The Bush Presidency: First Appraisals*, eds. Colin Campbell, S.J., and Bert A. Rockman. Chatham, New Jersey: Chatham House, 1991.

Beschloss, Michael R., and Thomas E. Cronin, eds. *Essays in Honor of James MacGregor Burns.* Englewood Cliffs, New Jersey: Prentice Hall, 1989.

Bessette, Joseph M., and Jeffrey Tulis, eds. "The Constitution, Politics, and the Presidency." *The Presidency in the Constitutional Order.* Baton Rouge: Louisiana State University Press, 1981.

Bibby, John F. *Politics, Parties, and Elections in America.* Chicago: Nelson Hall, 1987.

Biskupic, Joan. "Constitutional Questions Remain." *Congressional Quarterly* 49(2) (January 1991): 70.

Block, Fred, Richard Cloward, Barbara Ehrenreich, and Frances Fox Piven, eds. *The Mean Season.* New York: Pantheon, 1988.

Blumberg, Paul. *Inequality in an Age of Decline.* Oxford: Oxford University Press, 1980.

Bond, Jon R., and Richard Fleisher. *The President in the Legislative Arena.* Chicago: University of Chicago Press, 1990.

Broder, David S. "Bush: Quite a Communicator." *Washington Post*, May 30, 1990: A21.

Brogan, Hugh. *The Longman History of the United States of America.* New York: William Morrow, 1985.

Buchanan, Bruce. *The Citizen's Presidency.* Washington, D.C.: Congressional Quarterly Press, 1987.

Burke, John P. "Presidential Influence and the Budget Process: A Comparative Analysis," in *The Presidency and Public Policy Making*, eds. George C. Edwards III, Steven A. Shull, and Norman C. Thomas. Pittsburgh: University of Pittsburgh Press, 1985.

Burnham, Walter Dean, and Martha Wagner Weinberg, eds. *American Politics and Public Policy.* Cambridge, Massachusetts: MIT Press, 1978.

Burns, James MacGregor. *The Power to Lead: The Crisis of the American Presidency.* New York: Simon and Schuster, 1984.

_____. *Leadership*. New York: Harper and Row, 1978.

Burns, James MacGregor, J. W. Peltason, and Thomas E. Cronin. *Government by the People*, 13th National ed. Englewood Cliffs, New Jersey: Prentice Hall, 1987.

Bush, George. Quoted in Richard Rose, *The Postmodern President: George Bush Meets the World*, 2nd ed. Chatham, New Jersey: Chatham House, 1991.

Campbell S.J., Colin. *Managing the Presidency: Carter, Reagan, and the Search for Executive Harmony*. Pittsburgh: University of Pittsburgh Press, 1986.

Cannon, Lou. *President Reagan: The Role of a Lifetime*. New York: Simon and Schuster, 1991.

Chomsky, Noam. *Deterring Democracy*. London: Verso, 1991.

Chubb, John E., and Paul E. Peterson, eds. *The New Direction in American Politics*. Washington, D.C.: Brookings Institution, 1985.

Cloward, Richard, and Frances Fox Piven. *The New Class War*. New York: Pantheon, 1985.

Cohen, Richard E. "Marching Through the War Powers Act." *National Journal*. 52, December 30, 1989: 3120.

Coles, Robert. *Children of Crisis: A Study of Courage and Fear*. Boston: Little, Brown, 1967.

"Congress Reels Under Impact of Marine Deaths in Beirut, U.S. Invasion of Grenada." *Congressional Quarterly Weekly Report* 41(43), October 29, 1983: 2215-2218.

Corwin, Edward S. *The President: Office and Powers*, 4th ed. New York: New York University Press, 1957.

Crabb, Cecil V., Jr., and Pat M. Holt. *Invitation to Struggle: Congress, the President, and Foreign Policy*, 3rd ed. Washington, D.C.: Congressional Quarterly Press, 1989.

Cronin, Thomas E. "The Paradoxes of the Presidency," in *Analyzing the Presidency*, ed. Robert E. DeClerico. Guilford, Connecticut: Dushkin Publishing Group, 1985.

_____. *Rethinking the Presidency*. Boston: Little, Brown, 1982.

_____. *The State of the Presidency*, 2nd ed. Boston: Little, Brown, 1980.

Dahl, Robert. *A Preface to Democratic Theory*. Chicago: University of Chicago Press, 1956.

Dallek, Robert. *Ronald Reagan: The Politics of Symbolism*. Cambridge, Massachusetts: Harvard University Press, 1984.

DeClerico, Robert E., ed. *Analyzing the Presidency*. Guilford, Connecticut: Dushkin Publishing Group, 1985.

_____. *The American President*, 3rd ed. Englewood Cliffs, New Jersey: Prentice Hall, 1990.

Diggins, John Patrick. *The Lost Soul of American Politics: Virtue, Self-Interest, and the Foundations of Liberalism*. Chicago: University of Chicago Press, 1984.

Dillin, John. "Public Wants Bush to Shift Focus to Domestic Issues, Pollsters Say." *Christian Science Monitor*, July 25, 1991: 1.

Disch, Lisa M. "Toward a Feminist Conception of Politics." *PS: Political Science and Politics* 24(3) (September 1991): 501-504.

Draper, Theodore. *A Very Thin Line: The Iran-Contra Affairs*. New York: Hill and Wang, 1991.

Dryzek, John S. "The Mismeasure of Political Man." *The Journal of Politics* 50 (1988): 705-725.

Duffy, Michael. "Mr. Consensus," *Time.* August 21, 1989: 18-19.

Easton, David, and Jack Dennis, *Children in the Political System: Origins of Political Legitimacy.* New York: McGraw Hill, 1969.

Edelman, Murray. *Constructing the Political Spectacle.* Chicago: University of Chicago Press, 1988.

Edwards, George C. III. "George Bush and the Public Presidency: The Politics of Inclusion," in *The Bush Presidency: First Appraisals*, eds. Colin Campbell, S.J. and Bert A. Rockman. Chatham, New Jersey: Chatham House, Inc., 1991.

_____. "Nowhere to Go and No Way to Get There: Congressional Relations in the Early Bush Administration." *The Political Science Teacher* 2(3) (Summer 1989): 3.

_____. *At the Margins: Presidential Leadership of Congress.* New Haven: Yale University Press, 1989.

_____. "Preface: Presidential Policy Making," in *The Presidency and Public Policy Making*, eds. George C. Edwards III, Steven A. Shull, and Norman Thomas. Pittsburgh: University of Pittsburgh Press, 1985.

_____. *The Public Presidency: The Pursuit of Popular Support.* New York: St. Martin's Press, 1983.

Edwards, George C. III, Steven A. Shull, and Norman Thomas, eds. *The Presidency and Public Policy Making.* Pittsburgh: University of Pittsburgh Press, 1985.

Edwards, George C. III, and Stephen J. Wayne. *Presidential Leadership: Politics and Policy Making*, 2nd ed. New York: St. Martin's Press, 1990.

_____, eds. *Studying the Presidency.* Knoxville: University of Tennessee Press, 1983.

Elving, Ronald D. "The Changing Image of President Bush." *Congressional Quarterly Weekly Report*, June 2, 1990: 1758.

Etzioni, Amitai. "Today We Elect a President-Monarch." *New York Times*, November 8, 1988, p. A-23.

Evans, Sara M., and Harry C. Boyte. *Free Spaces: The Sources of Democratic Change in America.* New York: Harper and Row, 1986.

Falk, Richard. "Preface," in *The Iran-Contra Connection*, Jonathan Marshall, Peter Dale Scott, and Jane Hunter. Boston: South End Press, 1987.

Farr, James. "Political Science and the Enlightenment of Enthusiasm." *American Political Science Review*, 82(1), (March 1988): 51-71.

Farrand, Max, ed. *The Records of the Federal Convention of 1787*, 3 Vols. New Haven: Yale University Press, 1966.

Felton, John. "Bush, Hill Reach Agreement on Covert Action Issues." *Congressional Quarterly Weekly Report.* 47(43), October 28, 1989: 2884-2886.

_____. "In Wake of Libya, Skirmishing Over War Powers." *Congressional Quarterly Weekly Report.* 44(19), May 10, 1986: 1021-1024.

Ferguson, Thomas, and Joel Rogers, *Right Turn: The Decline of the Democrats and the Future of American Politics.* New York: Hill and Wang, 1986.

Fesler, James W. "The Brownlow Committee Fifty Years Later." *Public Administration Review*, July/August 1987: 292.

Finer, Herbert. *The Presidency: Crisis and Regeneration*. Chicago: University of Chicago Press, 1960.
Fiorina, Morris P. *Congress: The Keystone of the Washington Establishment*, 2nd ed. New Haven: Yale University Press, 1989.
_____. "The Presidency and Congress." *The Presidency and the Political System*, 2nd ed., ed. Michael Nelson. Washington, D.C.: Congressional Quarterly Press, 1988
Fisher, Louis. *The Politics of Shared Power: Congress and the Executive*. Washington, D.C.: Congressional Quarterly Press, 1987.
_____. *Constitutional Conflicts between Congress and the President*. Princeton, New Jersey: Princeton University Press, 1985.
_____. "The Doctrine of Separated Powers," in *Rethinking the Presidency*, ed. Thomas E. Cronin. Boston: Little, Brown, 1982.
Flacks, Richard. *Making History*. New York: Columbia University Press, 1988.
Franck, Thomas M. *The Tethered Presidency: Congressional Restraints on Executive Power*. New York: New York University Press, 1981.
Franklin, Daniel Paul. "War Powers in the Modern Context." *Congress and the Presidency* 14(1), (Spring 1987): 77-92.
Friedman, Thomas L. "Congress Generally Supports Attack, but Many Fear Consequences." *New York Times*, December 21, 1989: A21.
Gemma, Gavrielle, and Teresa Gutierrez. "Introduction," in *The U.S. Invasion of Panama: The Truth Behind Operation 'Just Cause.'* Prepared by the Independent Commission of Inquiry on the U.S. Invasion of Panama. Boston: South End Press, 1991.
Ginsberg, Benjamin, and Martin Shefter. "After the Reagan Revolution: A Postelectoral Politics," in *Looking Back on the Reagan Presidency*, ed. Larry Berman. Baltimore: Johns Hopkins University Press, 1990.
Gold, Allan R. " Environmentalists Dismayed by Bush's Nominees." *New York Times*, October 29, 1989: 33.
Goodgame, Dan. "Big Bad John Sununu." *Time*, May 21, 1990: 25.
Grant, Ruth Weissbourd, and Stephen Grant. "The Constitution, Politics, and the Presidency," in *The Presidency in the Constitutional Order*, eds. Joseph M. Bessette and Jeffrey Tulis. Baton Rouge: Louisiana State University Press, 1981.
Greenhouse, Linda. "Bill Would Give Reagan a Free Hand on Terror." *New York Times*, April 18, 1986: A9.
Greenstein, Fred I. "Nine Presidents: In Search of a Modern Presidency," in *Leadership in the Modern Presidency*, ed. Fred I. Greenstein. Cambridge, Massachusetts: Harvard University Press, 1988.
_____, ed. *Leadership in the Modern Presidency*. Cambridge, Massachusetts: Harvard University Press, 1988.
_____, ed. *The Reagan Presidency: An Early Assessment*. Baltimore: Johns Hopkins University Press, 1983.
_____. "What the President Means to Americans," in *Choosing the President*, ed. James David Barber. Englewood Cliffs, New Jersey: Prentice Hall, 1974.
Grossman, Michael Baruch, and Martha Joynt Kumar. *Portraying the President: The White House and the News Media*. Baltimore: Johns Hopkins University Press, 1981.

Grover, William F. *The President as Prisoner: A Structural Critique of the Carter and Reagan Years.* Albany: State University of New York Press, 1989.

Gutman, Roy. *Banana Diplomacy: The Making of American Policy in Nicaragua, 1981-1987.* New York: Simon and Schuster, 1988.

Gwertzman, Bernard. "An Invasion Prompted by Previous Debacles." *The New York Times,* October 26, 1983: A1.

_____. "Questions on Mission." *New York Times,* October 24, 1983: A1.

Habermas, Jurgen. *The Structural Transformation of the Public Sphere.* Cambridge: Cambridge University Press, 1989.

Haftendorn, Helga. "Toward a Reconstruction of American Strength: A New Era in the Claim to Global Leadership?" in *The Reagan Administration: A Reconstruction of American Strength?* eds. Helga Haftendorn and Jakob Schissler. Berlin: Walter de Guyer, 1988.

Haftendorn, Helga and Jacob Schissler, eds. *The Reagan Administration: A Reconstruction of American Strength?* Berlin: Walter de Guyer, 1988.

Hamilton, Alexander. "Federalist #22". *The Federalist Papers.* New York: New American Library, 1961.

_____. "Federalist #70." *The Federalist Papers.* New York: New American Library, 1961.

Harrington, Michael. *The New American Poverty.* Chicago: Henry Holt, 1984.

Hart, John. *The Presidential Branch.* Elmsford, New York: Pergamon, 1987.

_____. "The President and His Staff," in *The Modern Presidency: From Roosevelt to Reagan,* ed. Malcolm T. Shaw. New York: Harper and Row, 1987.

Heclo, Hugh. "Introduction: The Presidential Illusion," in *The Illusion of Presidential Government,* eds. Hugh Heclo and Lester M. Salamon. Boulder, Colorado: Westview Press, 1981.

Heclo, Hugh, and Lester M. Salamon, eds. *The Illusion of Presidential Government.* Boulder, Colorado: Westview Press, 1981.

Heilbroner, Robert L. *An Inquiry into the Human Prospect: Looked at Again for the 1990's.* New York: Norton, 1991.

Heineman, Ben W. "Some Rules of the Game: Prescription for Organizing the Domestic Presidency," in *The Presidency in Transition,* eds. James Pfiffner and R. Gordon Hoxie. New York: Center for the Study of the Presidency Proceedings, Vol. VI, No. 1, 1989.

Herson, Lawrence JR. *The Politics of Ideas: Political Theory and American Public Policy.* Homewood, Illinois: Dorsey Press, 1984.

Hertsgaard, Mark. *On Bended Knee: The Press and the Reagan Presidency.* New York: Farrar, Straus, and Giroux, 1988.

Hess, Stephen. *Organizing the Presidency,* 2nd ed. Washington: Brookings Institution, 1988.

Hess, Robert D., and Judith V. Torney. *The Development of Political Attitudes in Children.* Cited in Raymond Tatalovich and Byron W. Daynes, *Presidential Power in the United States.* Monterey, California: Brooks-Cole, 1985.

Hill, Leslie I. "Power and Citizenship in a Democratic Society," *PS: Political Science and Politics* 24(3), (September 1991): 495-498.

Hinckley, Barbara. *The Symbolic Presidency: How Presidents Portray Themselves.* New York: Routledge, Chapman and Hall, 1990.

_____. *Problems of the Presidency: A Text with Readings.* Glenview, Illinois: Scott Foresman, 1985.

Hodgson, Godfrey. *All Things to All Men.* New York: Simon and Schuster, 1980.

Hofstadter, Richard. "The Founding Fathers: An Age of Realism," in *The Moral Foundations of the American Republic,* 3rd ed., ed. Robert Horwitz. Charlottesville: University of Virginia Press, 1986.

_____. *The American Political Tradition.* New York: Alfred A. Knopf, 1948.

Horwitz, Robert, ed. *The Moral Foundations of the American Republic,* 3rd ed. Charlottesville: University of Virginia Press, 1986.

Jaros, Dean, Herbert Hirsch, and Federic J. Fleron, Jr. "The Malevolent Leader: Political Socialization in an American Sub-Culture." *American Political Science Review* 62 (June 1968): 564-65.

Jefferson, Thomas. Quoted in Donald L. Robinson, *"To the Best of My Ability:" The Presidency and the Constitution.* New York: Norton, 1987.

Jones, Charles, ed. *The Reagan Legacy: Promise and Performance.* Chatham, New Jersey: Chatham House, 1988.

_____. *The Trusteeship Presidency.* Baton Rouge: Louisiana State University Press, 1988.

Jones, Kathleen B. "Citizenship in a Woman-Friendly Polity" (review essay). *Signs: Journal of Women in Culture and Society,* 15(4), (1990): 781-812.

Kammen, Michael. *A Machine that Would Go By Itself: The Constitution in American Culture.* New York: Alfred A. Knopf, 1986.

Katz, Michael. *The Undeserving Poor.* New York: Pantheon, 1989.

Kellerman, Barbara. *The Political Presidency: Practice of Leadership.* New York: Oxford University Press, 1984.

Kellerman, Barbara, and Ryan J. Barilleaux. *The President as World Leader.* New York: St. Martin's Press, 1991.

Kernell, Samuel, *Going Public: New Strategies of Presidential Leadership.* Washington, D.C.: Congressional Quarterly Press, 1986, pp. 148-181.

_____. "Campaigning, Governing, and the Contemporary Presidency," in *The New Direction in American Politics,* eds. John E. Chubb and Paul E. Peterson. Washington, D.C.: Brookings Institution, 1985.

Kernell, Samuel, Peter W. Sperlich, and Aaron Wildavsky. "Public Support for Presidents," in *Perspectives on the Presidency,* ed. Aaron Wildavsky. Boston: Little, Brown, 1975.

Kessler, Frank. *The Dilemmas of Presidential Leadership: Of Caretakers and Kings.* Englewood Cliffs, New Jersey: Prentice Hall, 1982.

King, Gary W., and Lyn Ragsdale. *The Elusive Executive: Discovering Statistical Patterns in the Presidency.* Washington, D.C.: Congressional Quarterly Press, 1988.

Koh, Harold Hongju. "Why the President (Almost) Always Wins in Foreign Affairs: Lessons of the Iran-Contra Affair." *The Yale Law Journal* 97(7), (June 1988): 1258-1342.

Kosterlitz, Julie, and W. John Moore. "Saving the Welfare State," *National Journal,* 20 (May 14, 1988): 1276-1278+

Kozak, David C., and Kenneth N. Ciboski, eds. *The American Presidency: A Policy Perspective from Readings and Documents.* Chicago: Nelson Hall, 1985.

Leuchtenburg, William E. "Franklin D. Roosevelt: The First Modern President," in *Leadership in the Modern Presidency*, ed. Fred I. Greenstein. Cambridge, Massachusetts: Harvard University Press, 1988.

_____. *In the Shadow of FDR*. Ithaca: Cornell University Press, 1983.

Levin, Martin. "Ask Not What Our Presidents Are 'Really Like'; Ask What We and Our Political Institutions Are Like: A Call for a Politics of Institutions, Not Men," in *American Politics and Public Policy*, eds. Walter Dean Burnham and Martha Wagner Weinberg. Cambridge, Massachusetts: MIT Press, 1978.

Light, Paul C. *The President's Agenda: With Notes on Ronald Reagan*. Baltimore: Johns Hopkins University Press, 1983.

Lipset, Seymour Martin. *The First New Nation*. New York: Norton, 1979.

Lowi, Theodore J. "An Aligning Election: A Presidential Plebiscite," in *The Elections of 1984*, ed. Michael Nelson. Washington, D.C.: Congressional Quarterly Press, 1985.

_____. *The Personal President: Power Invested and Promise Unfulfilled*. Ithaca: Cornell University Press, 1985.

_____. *The End of Liberalism: The Second Republic of the United States*, 2nd ed. New York: Norton, 1979.

Mackenzie, G. Calvin. "Issues and Problems in the Staffing of New Administrations." *The Political Science Teacher* 2(3), (Summer 1989): 6.

_____. Quoted in Richard Nathan, *The Administrative Presidency*. New York: John Wiley and Sons, 1983.

_____. "The Paradox of Presidential Personnel Management," in *The Illusion of Presidential Government*, eds. Hugh Heclo and Lester M. Salamon. Boulder, Colorado: Westview Press, 1981.

Macpherson, C. B. *The Life and Times of Liberal Democracy*. Oxford: Oxford University Press, 1976.

Madison, Christopher. "Sideline Players." *National Journal*, 50 (December 15, 1990): 3024-3026.

_____. "Will Bush Ask for an OK Before War?" *National Journal*, 45 (November 10, 1990): 2751.

_____. "No Blank Check." *National Journal*, 40 (October 6, 1990): 2395-2398.

_____. "Bush's Breaks." *National Journal*, March 10, 1990, 564.

Madison, James. Quoted in Theodore Draper, *A Very Thin Line: The Iran-Contra Affairs*. New York: Hill and Wang, 1991.

_____. *Notes on Debates in the Federal Convention of 1787 Reported by James Madison*. New York: Norton, 1987.

_____. Quoted in Christopher H. Pyle and Richard M. Pious, *The President, Congress, and the Constitution*. New York: Free Press, 1984.

_____. "Federalist #75." *The Federalist Papers*. New York: New American Library, 1961.

_____. "Federalist #10." *The Federalist Papers*. New York: New American Library, 1961.

Mann, Thomas E. "Making Foreign Policy: President and Congress," in *A Question of Balance: The President, the Congress, and Foreign Policy*, ed. Thomas E. Mann. Washington, D.C.: Brookings Institution, 1990.

_____, ed. *A Question of Balance: The President, the Congress, and Foreign Policy.* Washington, D.C.: Brookings Institution, 1990.

Mansfield, Harvey C., Jr. *Taming the Prince: The Ambivalence of Modern Executive Power.* New York: Free Press, 1989.

Mason, Ronald M. *Participatory and Workplace Democracy: A Theoretical Development in the Critique of Liberalism.* Carbondale: Southern Illinois University Press, 1982.

McMahan, Jeff. *Reagan and the World: Imperial Policy in the New Cold War.* New York: Monthly Review Press, 1985.

Mervin, David. "The President and Congress," in *The Modern Presidency: From Roosevelt to Reagan,* ed. Malcolm Shaw. New York: Harper and Row, 1987.

Milkis, Sidney M., and Michael Nelson. *The American Presidency: Origins and Development, 1776-1990.* Washington, D.C.: Congressional Quarterly Press, 1990.

Miroff, Bruce. "Monopolizing the Public Space: The President as a Problem for Democratic Politics," in *Rethinking the Presidency,* ed. Thomas Cronin. Boston: Little, Brown, 1982.

Moe, Terry M. "The Politicized Presidency," in *The New Direction in American Politics,* eds. John E. Chubb and Paul E. Peterson. Washington, D.C.: Brookings Institution, 1985.

Mondale, Walter. Quoted in Samuel Kernell, "Campaigning, Governing, and the Contemporary Presidency," in *The New Direction in American Politics,* eds. John E. Chubb and Paul E. Peterson. Washington, D.C.: Brookings Institution, 1985.

Moore, W. John. "Hands Off." *National Journal,* 26 (July 1, 1989): 1678-1683.

Morris, Richard B. "The Origins of the American Presidency," in *Essays in Honor of James MacGregor Burns,* eds. Michael R. Beschloss and Thomas E. Cronin. Englewood Cliffs, New Jersey: Prentice Hall, 1989.

_____. *The Forging of the Union, 1781-1789.* New York: Harper and Row, 1989.

Muir, William K., Jr. "The Primacy of Rhetoric," in *Leadership in the Modern Presidency,* ed. Fred I. Greenstein. Cambridge, Massachusetts: Harvard University Press, 1988.

Myers, Minor, Jr. *Liberty Without Anarchy: A History of the Society of the Cincinnati.* Charlottesville: University of Virginia Press, 1983.

Nathan, Richard. *The Administrative Presidency.* New York: John Wiley and Sons, 1983.

_____. "The Reagan Presidency in Domestic Affairs," in *The Reagan Presidency: An Early Assessment,* ed. Fred I. Greenstein. Baltimore: Johns Hopkins University Press. 1983.

Nelson, Michael. "Evaluating the Presidency," in *The Presidency and the Political System,* 2nd ed., ed. Michael Nelson. Washington, D.C.: Congressional Quarterly Press, 1988.

_____, ed. *The Elections of 1984.* Washington, D.C.: Congressional Quarterly Press, 1985.

Neustadt, Richard E. *Presidential Power: The Politics of Leadership from FDR to Carter.* New York: John Wiley and Sons, 1980.

Oakes, John B. "Bush Nominates Watt II." *New York Times*, November 8, 1989.

Ophuls, William. *Ecology and the Politics of Scarcity*. San Francisco: W.H. Freeman, 1977.

Ost, David. *Solidarity and the Politics of Anti-Politics: Opposition and Reform in Poland Since 1968*. Philadelphia: Temple University Press, 1989.

Page, Benjamin I., and Mark P. Petracca. *The American Presidency*. New York: McGraw Hill, 1983.

Parker, Glenn R. *Characteristics of Congress: Patterns in Congressional Behavior*. Englewood Cliffs: Prentice Hall, 1989.

Pateman, Carole. *Participation and Democratic Theory*. Cambridge: Cambridge University Press, 1970.

Patterson, Bradley H. Jr., *The Ring of Power*. New York: Basic Books, 1988.

Pfaff, William. *Barbarian Sentiments: How the American Century Ends*. New York: Hill and Wang, 1989.

Pfiffner, James P. "Establishing the Bush Presidency." *Public Administration Review*, 50, (January/February 1990): 64-73.

_____. "Introduction: The Presidency in Transition," in *The Presidency in Transition*, eds. James P. Pfiffner and R. Gordon Hoxie. New York: Center for the Study of the Presidency Proceedings, Vol. VI, No. 1, 1989.

_____. *The Strategic Presidency*. Homewood, Illinois: Dorsey, 1987.

Pfiffner, James, and R. Gordon Hoxie, eds. *The Presidency in Transition*. New York: Center for the Study of the Presidency Proceedings, Vol. VI, No. 1, 1989.

Pika, Joseph A. "Reaching Out to Organized Interests: Public Liaison in the Modern White House," in *The Presidency Reconsidered*, ed. Richard Waterman. Itasca, Illinois: Peacock Press, forthcoming.

Pious, Richard M. *The American Presidency*. New York: Basic Books, 1979.

President's Committee on Administrative Management, *Administrative Management in the Government of the United States*. Washington, D.C.: U.S. Government Printing Office, 1937.

Pritchett, C. Herman. "The President's Constitutional Position," in *Rethinking the Presidency*, ed. Thomas E. Cronin. Boston: Little, Brown, 1982.

Pyle, Christopher H., and Richard M. Pious. *The President, Congress, and the Constitution*. New York: Free Press, 1984.

Reagan, Ronald. Quoted in Shirley Anne Warshaw, "Cabinet Government in the Modern Presidency," in *The Presidency in Transition*, eds. James P. Pfiffner and R. Gordon Hoxie. New York: Center for the Study of the Presidency Proceedings, Vol. VI, No. 1, 1989.

_____. Quoted in Julie Kosterlitz and W. John Moore, "Saving the Welfare State." *National Journal*, 20, (May 14,1988): 1276.

_____. Quoted in Donald L. Robinson, "*To the Best of My Ability*": *The Presidency and the Constitution*. New York: Norton, 1987.

Reinhard, Gregor. "The Origins of the Presidency," in *The American Presidency: A Policy Perspective from Readings and Documents*, eds. David C. Kozak and Kenneth N. Ciboski. Chicago: Nelson Hall, 1985.

Rimmerman, Craig A. "The 'Post-Modern' Presidency—A New Presidential Epoch? A Review Essay." *Western Political Quarterly*, 44(1), (March 1991).

Ripley, Randall B. *Congress: Process and Policy*, 4th ed. New York: Norton, 1988.

Roberts, Steven V. "Legislators Say Reagan Must Reassess U.S. Role." *New York Times*, October 24, 1983: A8.

_____. "Move in Congress." *New York Times*, October 28, 1983: A1.

Robinson, Donald L. *"To the Best of My Ability": The Presidency and the Constitution*. New York: Norton, 1987.

Rockman, Bert A. "Presidential and Executive Studies: The One, the Few, and the Many," in *Political Science: The Science of Politics*, ed. Herbert Weisberg. New York: Agathon Press, 1988.

Rose, Richard. *The Postmodern President: George Bush Meets the World*, 2nd ed. Chatham, New Jersey: Chatham House, 1991.

_____. *The Postmodern President: The White House Meets the World*. Chatham, New Jersey: Chatham House, 1991.

Rosenthal, Andrew. "Sununu Says Bush 'Ad-Libbed' Comment on Credit Card Rates." *New York Times*, November 23, 1991: A1.

Rossiter, Clinton. *1787: The Grand Convention*. New York: Norton, 1966.

_____. *The American Presidency*, revised ed. New York: Mentor, 1960.

Rourke, Francis. "Presidentializing the Bureaucracy." Paper prepared for the 1987 annual meeting of the American Political Science Association, Chicago, Illinois, September 3-6, 1987.

Salamon, Lester M., and Michael S. Lund. "Governing in the Reagan Era: An Overview," in *The Reagan Presidency and the Governing of America*, eds. Lester M. Salamon and Michael S. Lund. Washington, D.C.: Urban Institute Press, 1985.

_____, eds. *The Reagan Presidency and the Governing of America*. Washington, D.C.: Urban Institute Press, 1985.

Schick, Allen. *Reconciliation and the Congressional Budget Process*. Washington, D.C.: American Enterprise Institute, 1981.

Schissler, Jakob. "The Impact of the War Powers Resolution On Crisis Decision Making." in *The Reagan Administration: A Reconstruction of American Strength?* eds. Helga Haftendorn and Jakob Schissler. Berlin: Walter de Guyer, 1988.

Schlesinger, Arthur, Jr. *The Imperial Presidency*. Boston: Houghton Mifflin, 1973.

Seib, Gerald F. "Bush's Appointments Mark Him as a Man of the Establishment." *Wall Street Journal*, December 14, 1988: 1.

Seligman, Lester G., and Cary R. Covington. *The Coalitional Presidency*. Chicago: Richard Irwin, 1989.

Shannon, W. Wayne. "Mr. Reagan Goes to Washington: Teaching Exceptional America." *Public Opinion*, 4(6), (December-January 1982): 13-17, 58-60.

Sharpe, Kenneth E. "The Post-Vietnam Formula under Siege: The Imperial Presidency and Central America." *Political Science Quarterly*, 102(4), (Winter 1987-1988): 548-569.

Shaw, Malcolm. "The Traditional and Modern Presidencies," in *The Modern Presidency: From Roosevelt to Reagan*, ed. Malcolm Shaw. New York: Harper and Row, 1987.

_____, ed. *The Modern Presidency: From Roosevelt to Reagan*. New York: Harper and Row, 1987.

Sigel, Roberta. "Images of the American Presidency." *Midwest Journal of Political Science*, 10, (February 1966): 123-127.

Smith, Hedrick. *The Power Game*. New York: Simon and Schuster, 1988.

Solomon, Burt. "Bush Cultivates the Press Corps . . . Hoping for a Harvest of Good Will." *National Journal*, 18, (May 5, 1990): 1104-1105.

_____. "Vulnerable to Events." *National Journal*, 22, (January 6, 1990): 6-10.

_____. "A Tangle of Old Relationships." *National Journal*, 39, (September 30, 1989): 2418.

Stockman, David. *The Triumph of Politics*. New York: Harper and Row, 1986.

Stuckey, Mary E. *The President as Interpreter-in-Chief*. Chatham, New Jersey: Chatham House, 1991.

Sundquist, James L. *Constitutional Reform and Effective Government*. Washington, D.C.: Brookings Institution, 1986.

Tatalovich, Raymond, and Byron W. Daynes. *Presidential Power in the United States*. Monterey, California: Brooks/Cole, 1985.

Taubman, Philip. "Senators Suggest Administration Exaggerated Its Cuba Assessment." *New York Times*, October 30, 1983: A22.

Taylor, Stuart, Jr. "Legality of Grenada Attack Disputed." *New York Times*, October 26, 1983: A19.

Thomas, Norman C. "Studying the Presidency: Where and How Do We Go From Here?" *Presidential Studies Quarterly*, VII, (Fall 1977):169-175.

Tolchin, Martin. "Legislators Express Concern on the Operation's Future." *New York Times*, December 22, 1989: A20.

Towell, Pat, and John Felton. "Invasion, Noreiga Ouster Win Support on Capitol Hill." *Congressional Quarterly Weekly Report*, 47(51), (December 23, 1989): 3532-3535.

Tulis, Jeffrey K. *The Rhetorical Presidency*. Princeton, New Jersey: Princeton University Press, 1987.

Waterman, Richard W. *Presidential Influence and the Administrative State*. Knoxville: University of Tennessee Press, 1989.

_____. "Editor's Introduction," in *The Presidency Reconsidered*, ed. Richard Waterman. Itasca, Illinois: Peacock Press, forthcoming.

_____, ed. *The Presidency Reconsidered*. Itasca, Illinois: Peacock Press, forthcoming.

Wayne, Steven J. *The Road to the White House*, 2nd ed. New York: St. Martin's Press, 1984.

_____. "Approaches," in *Studying the Presidency*, eds. George C. Edwards and Stephen J. Wayne. Knoxville: University of Tennessee Press, 1983.

Weekly Compilation of Presidential Documents. Washington, D.C.: Office of the Federal Register, National Archives and Records Service, General Services Administration, March 11, 1985: 245.

Weinraub, Bernard. "Qaddafi is Warned." *New York Times*, April 16, 1986: A1.

Weisberg, Herbert, ed. *Political Science: The Science of Politics*. New York: Agathon Press, 1988.

Weisman, Steven R. "Reagan Signs Bill Allowing Marines to Stay in Beirut." *New York Times*, October 13, 1983: A1.

Weissbourd, Ruth, and Stephen Grant, "The Constitution, Politics, and the Presidency," in *The Presidency in the Constitutional Order*, eds. Joseph M. Bessette and Jeffrey Tulis. Baton Rouge: Louisiana State University Press, 1981.

West, William F., and Joseph Cooper. "The Rise of Administrative Clearance," in *The Presidency and Public Policy Making*, eds. George C. Edwards III, Steven A. Shull, and Norman Thomas. Pittsburgh: University of Pittsburgh Press, 1985.

White, John Kenneth. *The New Politics of Old Values*. Hanover, New Hampshire: University Press of New England, 1988.

Williams, Phil. "The President and Foreign Relations," in *The Modern Presidency: From Roosevelt to Reagan*, ed. Malcolm T. Shaw. New York: Harper and Row, 1987.

Williams, Robert. "The President and the Executive Branch," in *The Modern Presidency: From Roosevelt to Reagan*, ed. Malcolm T. Shaw. New York: Harper and Row, 1987.

Wills, Garry. *Explaining America: The Federalist*. Garden City, New York: Doubleday, 1981.

_____. *Inventing America: Jefferson's Declaration of Independence*. New York: Random House, 1979.

Wolin, Sheldon. *The Presence of the Past: Essays on the State and the Constitution*. Baltimore: Johns Hopkins University Press, 1989.

Woodward, Bob. *The Commanders*. New York: Simon and Schuster, 1991.

_____. *Veil: The Secret Wars of the CIA, 1981-1987*. New York: Simon and Schuster, 1987.

About the Book
and Author

The U.S. presidency has been characterized in a variety of ways—imperial, impossible, imperiled; personal, plural, postmodern—depending on the era and who was in office. In this book, Professor Rimmerman outlines the attributes of the *plebiscitary* presidency, a form of the office that dates from the FDR period but that has been most fully exploited by Ronald Reagan. By contrasting the Reagan and Bush administrations, the author points up the shortcomings of a presidency that operates by plebiscite and directs us toward a new standard for electing and evaluating presidents—one that insists on a respect for institutional limitations and effective citizen participation. Participatory democracy is essential to counter the dangers of trends toward "presidency by plebiscite" such as hero worship and direct tele-electronic democracy, which were illustrated by Ross Perot's appeal to the American public during the 1992 elections.

Craig A. Rimmerman is associate professor of political science at Hobart and William Smith Colleges and recipient of the 1992-1993 William A. Steiger Congressional Fellowship award.

Index